CALLING A TRUCE TO TERROR

Recent Titles in
Contributions in Political Science
Series Editor: Bernard K. Johnpoll

Ernest Evans

CALLING A
TRUCE
TO TERROR

THE AMERICAN
RESPONSE TO
INTERNATIONAL
TERRORISM

Contributions in Political Science, Number 29

GREENWOOD PRESS
WESTPORT, CONNECTICUT • LONDON, ENGLAND

Library of Congress Cataloging in Publication Data

Evans, Ernest, 1950-
  Calling a truce to terror.

  (Contributions in political science ; no. 29 ISSN
0147-1066)
  Bibliography: p.
  Includes index.
  1. Terrorism.   I. Title.   II. Title: American
response to international terrorism.   III. Series.
  HV6431.E9   301.6′33   78-22722
  ISBN 0-313-21140-X

Library of Congress Catalog Card Number: 78-22722
ISBN: 0-313-21140-X
ISSN: 0147-1066

First published in 1979

Greenwood Press, Inc.
51 Riverside Avenue, Westport, Connecticut 06880

Printed in the United States of America

10 9 8 7 6 5 4 3 2 1

Mankind must put an end to war, or war will put an end to mankind. So let us resolve that Dag Hammarskjöld did not live, or die, in vain. Let us call a truce to terror.

John F. Kennedy, *address at the United Nations, September 25, 1961*

To my sister, Margaret Ann Evans

CONTENTS

FIGURES

TABLES

PREFACE

The origins of my concern about terrorism lie in the troubled decade of the 1960s. I began high school as the first major commitment of U.S. troops was being sent to Vietnam, and I graduated from college as the last U.S. forces were leaving Indochina. The period of domestic upheaval in the United States that the Vietnam war helped to set in motion has instilled in me an interest in the politics of violent conflict that continues to the present day. The current work is a manifestation of that interest.

As in the case with any full-length book, the list of those to be thanked is too long for everyone to be mentioned by name. To note only a few: J. Bowyer Bell of Columbia University, Ithiel de Sola Pool of MIT, George Rathjens of MIT, and Samuel P. Huntington of Harvard all made significant contributions to the initial version of this book. The manuscript was typed by Delores Burton, and I am grateful for the good job she did. During the trying period of researching and writing this book, I was frequently given good advice by Revan Miles and Gertrude Cotts. I would like to extend special thanks to all the individuals I interviewed in the course of my research and writing; their patience with my questions is deeply appreciated. Finally, I would like to thank the University Consortium for World Order Studies, the MIT Arms Control Project, the International Studies Association, and the Earhart Foundation for the financial support they provided for the research on this volume.

ERNEST EVANS

PART I The Problem of International Terrorism

It's getting uncommonly easy to
kill people in large numbers, and
and first thing a principle does—
if it really is a principle—is
to kill somebody.

Lord Peter Wimsey in
Dorothy Sayers' *Gaudy Night*

chapter 1
INTRODUCTION

Inasmuch as studies of the phenomenon of terrorism have been consistently plagued by vague and polemical definitions, the first step is to define the subject matter. In general terms, terrorism can be defined as a strategy whereby violence is used to produce certain effects in a group of people so as to attain some political end or ends. One of the effects of such a strategy is often fear; however, there can be, and usually are, other effects.[1]

Both states seeking to maintain power and non-state actors trying to attain power can resort to the strategy of terrorism. In the contemporary world, where terrorist strategies are usually linked to non-state actors, it is often forgotten that the origin of this political term was the state terror of the so-called Reign of Terror in 1793-1794 during the French Revolution. In this particular stage of the French Revolution, Robespierre and the Committee on Public Safety executed thousands of members of the opposition to the revolution. The term has been applied to acts of other governments in later historical periods, most notably in the case of the Great Terror of Joseph Stalin from 1936 to 1938. A government that resorts to terrorism the way Robespierre or Stalin did has one basic purpose: to intimidate those who offer any opposition to their policies.

This book, however, will concentrate on the use of terror by revolutionary sub-state groups out of power rather than by states. This particular concentration stems solely from considerations of personal scholarly interest. It does not in any sense indicate that state terror is not a serious problem (the *Gulag Archipelago* of Aleksandr Solzhenitsyn powerfully and starkly illustrates the full horrors of state terrorism) or that terrorism by non-state actors is somehow worse than state terrorism. It is hoped that this book will provide an objective discussion of terror by non-state actors and of the response to this problem by the government of the United States.

* * *

Terrorism is a strategy whereby violence is used to produce certain effects upon a group of people. With special reference to substate terrorism, this strategy is one of four "ideal type" strategies whereby a group out of power can effect violent social change, the other three being coup d'etat, insurrection, and guerrilla warfare. Table I sketches out the characteristics of these four strategies. In order to fully elucidate the strategy of terrorism it is necessary to discuss in some detail each of these four strategies.

TABLE I.   *Strategies of Violent Social Change*

	TIME TAKEN	RELATIONSHIP WITH EXISTING ARMED FORCES	STATUS OF OLD REGIME
Coup d'etat	Short	Won over	Ousted
Insurrection	Short	Defeated	Ousted
Guerrilla war	Long	Defeated	Ousted
Terrorism	Long	Evaded	Coerced

Table I distinguishes among the four strategies by means of three variables: first, the amount of time taken for the violent change in government to have effect; second, the relationship of the group seeking power with the existing security forces; and third, the method in which the old regime's authority is destroyed. Some of the strategies are similar in one or two of these variables, but all differ from each other in at least one variable.

In the first strategy of violent social change in Table I, the coup d'etat, the existing armed forces are won over before or after the overthrow of the established government. The group attempting the coup may be wholly within the armed forces or may include elements outside these forces. The time involved in a coup is short, because if a government loses the support of its military and/or police, it ordinarily cannot defend itself. (There are exceptions to this generalization; for example, the Spanish republican government was able to mount a prolonged resistance effort against Franco and the Spanish army following the latter's coup in 1936.) In a successful coup the old regime and its supporters are ousted from power.

In recent decades the coup d'etat has been a highly effective means of achieving violent change. Examples of this strategy are legion. For example, in 1952 a group of Egyptian military officers, including Colonel Gamal Abdel Nasser, ousted King Farouk of Egypt; in 1963 the South Vietnamese military overthrew President Diem; and in 1973 the Chilean military destroyed the three-year-old Marxist government of Salvador Allende. In all three examples one can see the characteristics of coup d'etat: the time involved was short, lasting at most a few days; the change in power was accomplished by a subversion of the existing armed forces; and the authorities of the old regime were expelled from power—Farouk went into exile while Diem and Allende were killed. Table II records the number of coups and attempted coups in the world in the period 1945-1967.

TABLE II. *Number of Coups, 1945-1967*

	TOTAL NUMBER OF COUP ATTEMPTS	NUMBER OF SUCCESSFUL COUPS
Latin America	47	30
Middle East*	20	13
Africa	17	13
Asia	18	12
Europe	2	2
Totals	104	61

*Including Turkey and North Africa.
Source: Edward Luttwak, *Coup d'Etat: A Practical Handbook* (New York: Alfred A. Knopf, 1969), pp. 204-207.

The second strategy of violent social change is the insurrection. An insurrection is similar to a coup d'etat in that the time element is short (the time involved is usually somewhat longer than in the case of a coup, but still rather short as compared to the processes of guerrilla warfare and terrorism) and in that the authorities of the old regime are removed from power. However, the strategy of insurrection differs from that of the coup d'etat in that the security forces are defeated rather than co-opted by the forces of the insurgents.

The long revolutionary history of France illustrates the distinction between a coup d'etat and an insurrection. In the century following the great revolution of 1789-1799 there were major insurrections in France in 1830, 1848, and 1871. In 1830 there was an uprising in Paris by the working class and the bourgeoisie against the Bourbon government of Charles X; the royal troops were defeated, and the king fled the country. The successor to Charles X, Louis Philippe, was overthrown by an insurrection of the workers of Paris in 1848; he too fled into exile. In 1871, in the aftermath of France's defeat at the hands of Prussia, the working class of Paris tried to set up a revolutionary republic, but the population and the armed forces for the most part remained loyal to the government, so after a bitterly fought siege the Paris Commune was defeated. In all three insurrections the time element was short, taking only a few months at most. In the case of the successful insurrections, those of 1830 and 1848, the existing governments of Charles X and Louis Philippe were ousted from power by physical force. And finally, in contrast to the coup d'etat, an attempt was made by the insurgents, successfully in 1830 and 1848 and unsuccessfully in 1871, to defeat rather than subvert the existing armed forces

The third strategy, guerrilla warfare, differs from a coup d'etat in two respects: the time element is long and the forces of the status quo are defeated rather than won over. It differs from insurrections in that the time element is prolonged: guerrillas start in a position of weakness and gradually wear down the opposition after an extended struggle. The post-World War II period has witnessed a number of successful guerrilla campaigns.[2] Two of the most famous culminated in 1949 when Mao Tse-tung and his guerrilla forces came to power in China after a more than twenty-year struggle against the Kuomintang and Chiang K'ai-shek and in 1954 when Ho Chi Minh secured French withdrawal from Indochina after an eight-year struggle.

The terrorism strategy differs in certain respects from all three of the above-mentioned strategies of violent social change. Unlike a coup d'etat or an insurrection, time is prolonged. Unlike the other three strategies, the existing armed forces are not won over or defeated; they are evaded. And finally, a sub-state actor using the strategy of terrorism seeks to accomplish the desired policy changes by coercing those in power rather than by removing them.

The strategy of terrorism has been resorted to frequently in the twentieth century. For example, in Ireland, following the failure of the 1916 Easter insurrection, the Irish Republican Army reorganized and in 1918-1921 unleashed a wave of attacks on British military and police targets. By 1921 the British were weary of the struggle and conceded the south of Ireland dominion status. In 1969-1970, after several abortive campaigns, the IRA began the present campaign to drive the British out of Ulster. Both these campaigns were prolonged: the first took from 1918 to 1921, and the second has gone on for nine years with no end in sight. In neither campaign did the IRA attempt to defeat the British army and police; rather it merely sought to evade these forces. And in both campaigns the IRA sought to destroy the authority of the old regime not by removing those in power but by coercing them—by making the costs of continuing the struggle too high to be worthwhile.

It must be emphasized that all these strategies of violent social change are "ideal types"; quite often a group seeking social and political change through violence will employ two, three, or even all four of the strategies mentioned above simultaneously. In the case of the Bolshevik seizure of power in 1917-1921, the November 1917 revolution in Petrograd was a cross between a coup d'etat and an insurrection. V. I. Lenin overthrew the government of Aleksandr Kerensky partially by winning over many of the troops of the Petrograd garrison, the classic strategy of coup, and partially by building up his own force of armed workers called the Red Guards, the strategy of insurrection. However, Lenin failed to co-opt enough of the armed forces to assume complete power, and consequently the Bolsheviks had to fight a civil war. In this civil war Lenin and his followers made frequent usé of both terrorism and guerrilla warfare.

This book is primarily concerned with international terrorism, that is, terrorist acts of international significance. The following set of conditions have to be met:

A. The act must be committed either against the nationals of one country outside of that country's borders or by a foreigner within a country's territory.
B. The purpose of the act must be explicitly political.
C. The motive of the act must be to damage the interests of or to obtain concessions from a government, an international company, or an international organization.

It might be noted in passing that one of the greatest difficulties in dealing with the problem of international terrorism is that it is so hard to obtain agreement among the community of nations on the boundaries of the problem. To briefly mention two of the major controversies:

A. Are acts of violence committed by infiltrators in colonial territories acts of international terrorism? When Portugal was waging its wars in Africa, it claimed that Angola, Mozambique, and Portuguese Guinea were merely overseas provinces of Portugal. Hence any acts of violence committed in these overseas provinces by outside elements were acts of international terrorism. The African states supporting the insurgencies in Portuguese Africa replied that Portugal was illegally holding onto its African territories in defiance of repeated United Nations resolutions. Thus any violent acts in these territories were not terrorism but rather legitimate acts of national self-determination.
B. Who is a foreigner? Arabs often claim that the Palestinian Arabs who carry out acts of violence in Israel are not foreigners attacking the citizens of another state (and hence perpetrators of acts of international terrorism) but rather are the legitimate residents of Palestine who have returned to fight for their homeland.

Here the basic focus will be on American efforts to develop a structure of deterrence against terrorist attacks on American diplomats and other citizens outside the territorial boundaries of the

United States. Certain categories of terrorist incidents have been excluded. The question of the deterrence of aerial hijacking is dealt with only indirectly: first, anti-hijacking law and treaties have already been dealt with in great detail by other authors[3] and, second, anti-hijacking law is a complicated topic more appropriately examined by an international lawyer.

The time period of this book will be from 1969 to the fall of 1978. On September 4, 1969, Charles Burke Elbrick, the American ambassador to Brazil, was kidnapped by a group of Brazilian terrorists. He was released after the Brazilian government flew fifteen prisoners to Mexico. This incident was chosen as the beginning of the study because after this kidnapping the United States began to formulate a policy toward acts of internationational terrorism. Prior to Elbrick's abduction there was no real policy because there had been few acts of transnational terrorism involving Americans.

* * *

The basic focus will be on efforts to deter acts of international terrorism directed against Americans. Specifically, there will be an analysis of deterrence efforts in both the area of what Martha Hutchinson of Wesleyan University calls "dual-phase" acts of terrorism (i.e., kidnappings) and in the area of what she calls "single-phase" acts of terrorism (i.e., shootings and bombings that do not involve the taking of hostages).[4] American attempts to deter political kidnappings have centered around the policy of "no concessions" to those holding Americans hostage, and therefore the deterrent effect of this policy will be evaluated. The American efforts to deter single-phase acts of terrorism have involved trying to get multilateral conventions against international terrorism passed and ratified, and so the main American effort in this regard, the 1972 Draft United Nations Convention on International Terrorism, will be discussed in detail.

Finally, brief mention should be made of one topic that this book will not deal with: there will not be any systematic evaluation of the normative questions involved in international terrorism. This omission should not be taken to signify that such questions are unimportant. They are very important and deserve careful study. However, to attempt to evaluate both normative and empirical questions in the space of a single book would be to take on an excessively large topic. So the choice was made to put normative concerns off to one side and to do an empirical evaluation of the phenomenon of transnational terrorism. It is hoped that a better understanding of empirical issues also will lead to a better grasp of the serious moral issues involved in this phenomenon.

NOTES

1. Brian Jenkins, *International Terrorism: A New Mode of Conflict* (Los Angeles: Crescent Publications, 1975), p. 1.

2. There also have been a vast number of unsuccessful guerrilla campaigns in recent decades, a point made by J. Bowyer Bell in his book *The Myth of the Guerrilla* (New York; Alfred A. Knopf, 1971), passim.

3. See, for example, Nancy Douglas Joyner, *Aerial Hijacking as International Crime* (Dobbs Ferry, New York: Oceana Publications, Inc., 1974) and Alona E. Evans, "Aircraft Hijacking: What Is Being Done," *American Journal of International Law*, Vol. 67, No. 4 (October 1973), pp. 641-671.

4. Martha Crenshaw Hutchinson, "Transnational Terrorism as a Policy Issue." Paper presented at the 1974 Annual Meeting of the American Political Science Association.

chapter 2

THE CAUSES OF
TERRORISM

Terrorism used as a strategy by groups out of power to attain their goals has a long history, as old as warfare itself. Thomas Schelling in *Arms and Influence* documents how the use of violence to terrorize and intimidate is an ancient tactic. He notes examples of violence used in this way in the wars between the Greeks and the Persians.[1] The all too prevalent idea that terrorism is a totally novel phenomenon is a myth. However, while terrorism has a long history, the current wave of this form of violence has been given impetus by a series of new developments in the post-World War II period. Any analysis of terrorism in the contemporary world must begin with a discussion of these developments.

The great majority of the nations of the world are undergoing a process of drastic social, economic, and political change that in the language of social science may be called "modernization." To understand the relationship of this process of modernization to terroristic violence, the concept of "relative deprivation" must be mentioned. Ted Robert Gurr in *Why Men Rebel* has argued that political violence is a consequence of a significant gap developing between the value expectations of a given group of people and the value capabilities of the group. Figures I, II, and III show the three possible patterns of relative deprivation.[2] "Decremental deprivation" (Figure I) occurs when the value capabilities of a given population decline drastically due to one or several national disasters. Gurr

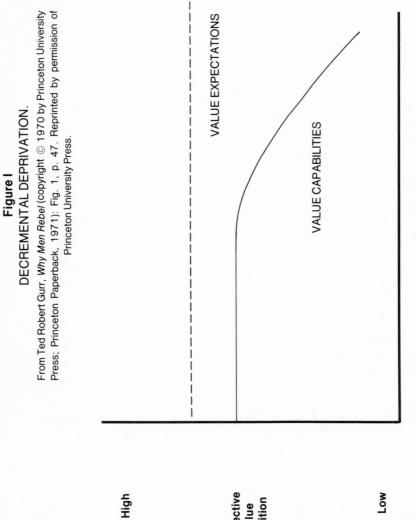

Figure I

DECREMENTAL DEPRIVATION.

From Ted Robert Gurr, *Why Men Rebel* (copyright © 1970 by Princeton University Press; Princeton Paperback, 1971): Fig. 1, p. 47. Reprinted by permission of Princeton University Press.

VALUE EXPECTATIONS

VALUE CAPABILITIES

Time

High

Collective Value Position

Low

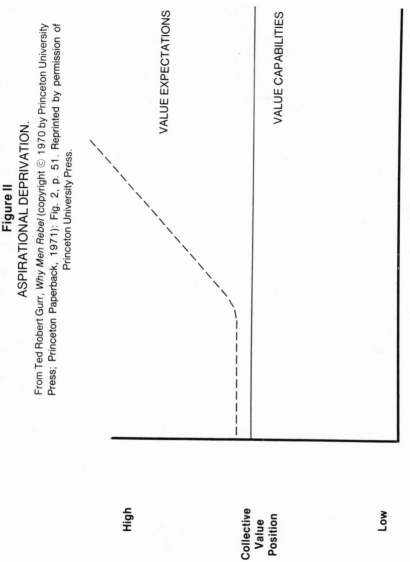

Figure II
ASPIRATIONAL DEPRIVATION.

From Ted Robert Gurr, *Why Men Rebel* (copyright © 1970 by Princeton University Press; Princeton Paperback, 1971): Fig. 2, p. 51. Reprinted by permission of Princeton University Press.

VALUE EXPECTATIONS

VALUE CAPABILITIES

Time

High

Collective
Value
Position

Low

Figure III

PROGRESSIVE DEPRIVATION.

From Ted Robert Gurr, *Why Men Rebel* (copyright © 1970 by Princeton University Press; Princeton Paperback, 1971): Fig. 3, p. 53. Reprinted by permission of Princeton University Press.

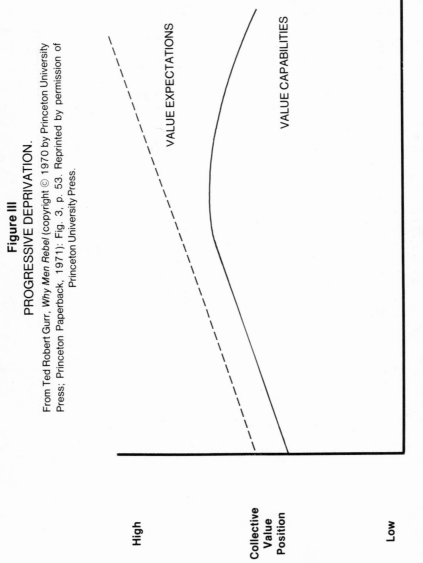

argues that the success of the Bolsheviks in seizing power in Russia in 1917 was due in large part to decremental deprivation: the enormous material and human sacrifices of the Russian people in World War I had created widespread discontent, and the failure of the Kerensky government to terminate Russian involvement in the war led to a swing in popular sentiment to the one group that promised immediate peace, namely, Lenin and his party.[3]

"Aspirational deprivation" (Figure II) occurs when the value capabilities of a group remain constant while its value expectations increase. Gurr points to the violence by black Americans in the 1960s as an example of violence caused by aspirational deprivation: black demands for immediate equality had come up against the realities of continuing discrimination and prejudice, resulting in widespread dissatisfaction and frustration.[4]

"Progressive deprivation" (Figure III) occurs when value capabilities stabilize or decline after a period in which value capabilities and value expectations have increased together. As an example of progressive deprivation Gurr notes the waves of rioting in colonies when liberalizing tendencies and reforms did not result in prompt independence.[5]

The process of modernization almost inevitably leads to widespread feelings of relative deprivation. Samuel P. Huntington has argued that during modernization the isolation of various ethnic groups from each other is broken down. These new contacts between groups lead them to compare, unfavorably, their share in values such as wealth, power, and knowledge with those of other groups. Modernization, Huntington argues, also produces feelings of relative deprivation by changing the relationship between communal groups in different societies: a previously dominant group may find its position threatened by another group that is better able to take advantage of the social and political changes taking place.[6] These pervasive feelings of relative deprivation in modernizing countries manifest themselves in all four forms of political violence outlined in the introduction: coup d'etats, insurrections, guerrilla wars, and terrorism are endemic among these nations.

A second factor that has contributed to the current wave of terrorism is what is often called the "ethnicity explosion." This factor

is related to the problem of modernization in that rapid socioeco-
nomic change engenders personal insecurity, which leads to a
search for an identity that cannot be changed by economic conditions. Such an identity is usually ascriptive (racial, ethnic, or religious).[7] In the 1960s violence among ethnic, racial, and religious
groups began an upward swing that has continued into the 1970s.
The principal manifestations of this violence have occurred in areas
which have been the meeting places of major cultures or races:[8]

A. Malays and Chinese: Malaysia, the Philippines, Thailand, and Indonesia.
B. Blacks and whites: Rhodesia, South Africa, Portuguese Africa, and the
    United States.
C. Latin versus Northern Europeans: Belgium and Canada.
D. Blacks and East Indians: Guyana, Trinidad, Uganda, Tanzania, and
    Kenya.
E. The Islamic world and the non-Islamic world: Nigeria, Cameroon,
    Ethiopia, Chad, Sudan, India-Pakistan, Thailand, the Philippines and
    the Israeli-Arab dispute.

A number of the terrorist and guerrilla movements of the past
decade grew out of these clashes across what Huntington calls the
"demographic faults of human civilization."[9] The Palestinian *fedayeen*
grew out of the clash between Jews and Arabs over Palestine. The
Front de Libération du Quebec (FLQ) arose from tensions between
French and English Canada. And the Eritrean Liberation Front was
a result of the conflict between Christians and Muslims in Ethiopia.

A third important factor is the influence of Frantz Fanon. Fanon,
a psychiatrist who served with the FLN in Algeria, wrote a book
entitled *The Wretched of the Earth* which has circulated widely
among contemporary revolutionary groups. Gustave Morf, a
Canadian psychiatrist who conducted a number of in-depth interviews with captured members of the FLQ, reported that they were
avid readers of *The Wretched of the Earth*.[10] Sir Geoffrey Jackson,
the former British ambassador to Uruguay who was kidnapped by
the Tupamaro guerrillas in January 1971 and held until the following
September, stated that the reading material of the Tupamaros
included a number of copies of *The Wretched of the Earth*.[11]

General Y. Harkabi, an Israeli scholar who has written extensively
on Arab attitudes toward Israel and has made a special study of the

attitudes and ideology of the Palestinian movement, has noted that the al Fatah pamphlet entitled *The Revolution and Violence, The Road to Victory* is a selective précis of *The Wretched of the Earth.* Harkabi argues that Fanon's influence is clear in a number of the other publications of the Palestinian movement.[12] Holden Roberto, the founder of the Frente Nacional de Liberatęcão de Angola— National Front for the Liberation of Angola (FNLA)—was heavily influenced both by Fanon's writings and by Fanon personally. When Roberto was in the process of laying the groundwork of the FNLA, he held extensive conversations with Fanon in Ghana while the author was there to represent the Algerian FLN.[13] Sean Holly, the American labor attaché who was kidnapped by a Guatemalan terrorist group called the Fuerzas Armadas Rebeldes—Rebel Armed Forces (FAR)—and released after the Guatemalan government turned over two political prisoners to the Costa Rican embassy, mentioned in an interview that the reading material of the FAR included *The Wretched of the Earth* along with works by Ché Guevara and Carlos Marighella.[14]

Clearly Fanon has had a major impact on contemporary revolutionary ideology. His writing has increased the acceptabilty of the strategy of terrorism for the following basic reason: Fanon argues that violence qua violence is useful and productive, *regardless* of whether violence actually moves the revolutionary movement any closer to its goals. Fanon advances two reasons why violence is constructive for oppressed people. First, he argues that violence has a positive impact on individuals. He maintains that at the level of the individual violence is a cleansing force that frees the native from his inferiority complex and makes him fearless. A people that has taken part in a violent struggle for national liberation will be jealous of the results of their action and will refuse to allow their destiny to be placed in hands of so-called "liberators."[15] Second, he argues that at the level of the community violence has a positive impact because it raises national consciousness. The practice of violence, Fanon claims, mobilizes an oppressed people and binds them together into a new nation.[16]

Fanon's arguments about the benefits of violence appear to have convinced many of his readers that they should not worry about whether or not such violence will help them attain their goals—

simply by using violence they will achieve something positive.
Thus one of the major arguments against terrorism, that from a
tactical point of view it is ineffective and even counterproductive
(the Marxist-Leninist position of orthodox communists), can be
quite forcefully countered. The result has been a growing accept-
ability of the strategy of terrorism among those who seek social and
political change.

The experience of decolonization has been a fourth factor
contributing to the current wave of terrorism. In an article entitled
"The Ecology of Terrorism," D. V. Segre and J. H. Alder argue that
the reason why many governments take a rather indulgent attitude
toward terrorism is that terrorism is frequently seen as a manifestation of the political and ideological struggles against imperialism
and colonialism. Given that a sizable majority of the world's
nations are products of the post-World War II decolonization
process, any group of movements seen as anticolonial can count on
considerable sympathy.[17]

Alder and Segre contend that the result of this sympathy is that
punishment for terrorists has been lenient for the most part. A RAND
Corporation study of 63 major hostage-taking incidents from 1968
to 1974 supports this contention. This study found that in these
situations there was a 79 percent chance that *all* members of the
terrorist team would escape punishment or death.[18] This governmental tolerance toward terrorism, Alder and Segre argue, has
created an international climate conducive to terrorist activities.[19]

A fifth factor is what J. Bowyer Bell calls "The Myth of the Guerrilla." This myth, stated succinctly, is that any movement that
employs the strategies of guerrilla warfare and/or terrorism is
assured of success. Bell argues that this belief has arisen because of
the success of a number of guerrilla movements in the post-World
War II period: Mao Tse-tung's communists in China, the FLN in
Algeria, Ho Chi Minh and the Viet Minh in Indochina, EOKA in
Cyprus, and the Zionist Underground in Palestine. Because of the
myth of the inevitability of success for those who use such strategies,
Bell maintains that the number of movements resorting to guerrilla
warfare and terrorism has gone up sharply in recent decades.[20]

In reality, Bell argues, the success of an underground movement
is by no means assured. There are several preconditions that have
to be met before a revolutionary movement can hope to achieve its

goals. First, there is the need for a sufficiently valid cause that can mobilize a core of militants without alienating the mass of the public. It is not necessary to achieve active public support; toleration is sufficient. But even toleration requires that the cause of the rebels have a sufficient degree of legitimacy in the eyes of the population.[21]

Second, the revolutionary movement must have some legitimacy in the eyes of the opposition. Of course, if the movement is capable of achieving a military victory over its opponents, then the perception of the insurgents in the eyes of the status quo is irrelevant; but such a capability is beyond the resources of many groups. As was noted in the typology in the introductory chapter, a terrorist strategy depends for success on coercing the opposition, not on defeating it by physical force. For such coercion to work the side using it must be less than totally unacceptable to the authorities; otherwise the conflict will go on.[22]

Third, the revolutionary organization must be able to raise the price of continuing the struggle to a point at which those resisting the organization will no longer be willing to pay and consequently will agree to give in.[23] There is, of course, no fixed price that represents the tolerance point of those in authority; the tolerance point varies greatly depending on what is being asked. For example, the British left South Yemen after having been subject to far less coercion than they have undergone in Ulster since 1969. The reason is simple: it is one thing to abandon a distant remnant of a vanished empire and quite another to abandon an integral part of the realm.

Certainly belief in the "myth" has not brought universal success. In the early 1960s, following the victory of Castro's forces in Cuba, there were predictions that a wave of rural-based insurgencies would spread revolutions throughout Latin America. Two decades later a chief prophet of rural guerrilla warfare in Latin America, Ché Guevara, is dead and with him the hopes of many Latin American revolutionaries for rural-based revolutions. These rural-based revolutionaries were defeated by a number of factors, including improved governmental counter-insurgency techniques, internal splits and infighting among the revolutionary movements, and an inability of the largely middle-class and city-raised revolutionaries to relate to the peasantry.[24] The Palestinian movement, which is frequently pointed to as an example of a movement that has successfully used terrorism, owes what victories it has achieved at least as much to the fact that it has powerful friends, namely, the Arab oil-producing states. Contrast the success of the Palestinian movement in attaining international recognition and support and in seemingly moving closer to its goals with the situation of the Kurds. The Kurds, like the Palestinians, are a Middle Eastern ethnic group that wants its own nation. They have been fighting off and on with a costly lack of success for over sixty years for independence from the three nations that divide their homeland: Iraq, Iran, and Turkey. The very different degrees of success between the Kurds and the Palestinians in attaining their goals are best explained by an old Kurdish proverb: "Kurds have no friends."[25]

Examples can be multiplied of unsuccessful guerrilla and terrorist movements, but the basic point remains the same: the use of guerrilla and terrorist strategies can lead to success only in certain instances. If the right conditions are not present, instead of a successful revolution you have either an indefinite stalemate or the defeat of the revolutionary organization.

A sixth factor is the impact of new technologies. Terrorist groups have skillfully exploited technological advances in the areas of transportation and communication. The world airways network has provided terrorists with a number of opportunities. Even a single individual can seize an airliner and have hundreds of hostages at his or her disposal. The hijacked aircraft offers a means of escape to any country that will provide sanctuary. The existence of air travel makes possible the development of an international network of contacts among various terrorist groups. And the ability of news agencies to broadcast around the world scenes from a terrorist incident via television and radio has given terrorists a means of attaining a vast amount of publicity.

Finally, there are the difficulties faced by the intelligence communities in responding to transnational terrorism. Miles Copeland in *Beyond Cloak and Dagger: Inside the CIA* notes three key difficulties:

A. There is no single international organization susceptible to penetration by undercover agents. Instead, there are a host of generally rather small terrorist organizations.

B. Only a very small number of the members of contemporary extremist organizations are agents of foreign powers. Usually the number of foreign agents in any given extremist group is less than one in a hundred. Sorting out that one foreign agent from the other ninety-nine members of the group so as to undercut the group's foreign assistance is a costly security operation.

C. The current wave of terrorism, which is mostly of an extreme leftist variety, is harder to contain than terrorism by nationalist rightist extremists because many militant leftists have decided that anyone or anything that aids "capitalism and imperialism" is a legitimate target. The rightist extremists are generally more selective, and hence it is easier to protect against their attacks.[26]

NOTES

1. Thomas C. Schelling, *Arms and Influence* (New Haven: Yale University Press, 1966), Chapter 1, pp. 1-34, passim.

2. Robert Ted Gurr, *Why Men Rebel* (Princeton, New Jersey: Princeton University Press, 1971), Chapters 2 and 3, passim.

3. Ibid., p. 49.

4. Ibid., p. 51.

5. Ibid., p. 53-54.

6. Samuel P. Huntington, "Civil Violence and the Process of Development," in *Civil Violence and the International System* (London: International Institute for Strategic Studies, 1971), pp. 11-12.

7. Ibid., pp. 11-12.

8. Ibid., p. 11.

9. Ibid., pp. 10-11.

10. Gustave Morf, *Terror in Quebec* (Toronto, Canada: Clarke, Irwin & Company Limited, 1970), p. 35.

11. Interview No. 9 (Sir Geoffrey Jackson).

12. Y. Harkabi, *Fedayeen Action and Arab Strategy* (London: International Institute for Strategic Studies, 1968), p. 14.

13. J. Bowyer Bell, *The Myth of the Guerrilla* (New York: Alfred A. Knopf, 1971), p. 114.

14. Interview No. 33 (Sean Holly).

15. Frantz Fanon, *The Wretched of the Earth* (New York: Grove Press, 1966), p. 73.

16. Ibid., p. 73.

17. D. V. Segre and J. H. Alder, "The Ecology of Terrorism," *Survival*, Vol. XV, No. 4 (July/August 1973), p. 179.

18. Central Intelligence Agency, *International and Transnational Terrorism: Diagnosis and Prognosis* (Washington, D.C.: CIA, 1976), p. 22.

19. Segre and Alder, "Ecology," p. 179.

20. Bell, *Myth*, passim.

21. Ibid., p. 52.

22. Ibid., pp. 53-54.

23. Ibid., p. 57.

24. Walter Laqueur, *Guerrilla* (Boston: Little, Brown & Company, 1976), pp. 315-319.

25. Ibid., pp. 307.

26. Miles Copeland, *Beyond Cloak and Dagger: Inside the CIA* (New York: Pinnacle Books, 1975), pp. 82-83. Copeland has been a long-time associate of many of the top people in the American intelligence community.

chapter 3
THE STRATEGY OF TERRORISM

Despite its long history, the strategy of terrorism has often been controversial, and in the past one hundred years there has been a continuing debate among revolutionaries as to the effectiveness and morality of terrorism. Karl Marx and Friedrich Engels had mixed feelings about terrorism. On the one hand, they were suspicious of many nineteenth-century terrorist movements because they felt the movement leaders erroneously believed that a conspiracy of a few individuals could overthrow a government. On the other hand, Marx and Engels showed considerable admiration for the Narodniki, the nineteeth-century Russian terrorists who assassinated Czar Alexander II in 1881. In response to criticism of the Narodniki, Engels stated that they were the only people doing anything to bring down the Czarist autocracy.[1]

In the years around the turn of the century there was a major discussion among revolutionaries in Russia on the use of terrorism. V. I. Lenin and Leon Trotsky both attacked the rival Social Revolutionaries for advocating terrorism. Lenin argued against individual terrorism on two grounds. The first was that a strategy of terrorism distracted desperately needed personnel from the main task of a revolutionary movement, namely, the organization of the working class. Lenin maintained that terrorism as it was practiced and preached by the Social Revolutionaries was not in any way linked to work among the masses. He stated that he was not opposed to terrorism on principle, but felt that terrorism should be one instrument of a broad revolutionary strategy. The problem with the Social Revolutionaries' use of terrorism was that instead of using terrorism as one instrument among many, they were using it as a panacea for all of their difficulties as a revolutionary organization.[2]

Lenin's second argument against individual terrorist acts was that such acts were a submission to what he called "spontaneity" rather than to "consciousness." To give a really complete description of how Lenin saw these two concepts would require a very long disgression. Basically, however, to Lenin the trouble with the Russian revolutionary movement in 1902 when he wrote his famous "What Is to Be Done" (where the two concepts were introduced) was that the movement emphasized the unorganized and unstructured aspects of class struggle (spontaneity) rather than a disciplined, organized mass movement to carry on this struggle (consciousness). Lenin believed that the terrorists in the Social Revolutionaries were simply passionately indignant intellectuals who were characterized by the "spontaneity" of which he was so critical. He felt that such intellectuals lacked the ability to connect the Russian revolutionary movement and the working class into an integrated, functioning revolutionary organization.[3]

Trotsky, like Lenin, argued against the use of individual terror. He also had two basic arguments against individual terrorism. The first was that terrorism did not disrupt the ruling class, but did disorganize the workers. Trotsky acknowledged that a successful terrorist incident could throw the ruling class into confusion, but he maintained that such confusion would inevitably be short-lived because the capitalist state is not based on individuals. The class structure would survive a terrorist attack, and this structure could replace any assassinated minister or leader. What a terrorist incident did do, Trotsky argued, was belittle all of the hard work of building up a powerful revolutionary movement. The spectacular nature of terrorist incidents caused people to forget that a successful revolution required a disciplined party capable of organizing meetings, carrying out mass agitation, and contesting elections. In short, Trotsky believed that terrorism distracted members of the working class from the need to put together a revolutionary movement and instead caused them to hope for salvation from an individual or a few individuals engaging in terrorism.[4]

Trotsky's second argument against terrorism was that if a revolutionary movement practiced individual terror, then inevitably the movement would become subordinate to the terrorist arm. He claimed that no matter where in the party hierarchy the terrorist arm was placed, in actual fact this arm would inevitably come to be above the party and all its work. He further argued that not only would the practice of terrorism subordinate the party to the terrorist arm of the party, but also that the police would find it easy to infiltrate and control the terrorist arm and thus would be in control of the party. In this connection Trotsky noted how the terrorist organization of the Social Revolutionaries had come under the control of Yevno Azef, an agent of the Czarist secret police.[5]

It should be noted that the Bolsheviks were opposed to what they called "individual terrorism," that is, what the introductory chapter of this book referred to as terrorism by non-state actors. Once in power they had no ideological objection to the use of state terror to intimidate their opponents. On the contrary, as the *Gulag Archipelago* of Aleksandr Solzhenitsyn documents in graphic and tragic detail, in consolidating their power the Bolsheviks used terror to an extent that has few parallels in human history.

Down to the present, orthodox Marxist-Leninists have echoed the strictures of Trotsky and Lenin against the use of terror as a strategy to seize power. Ché Guevara condemned the use of terrorism in his book on guerrilla war. He argued that terrorism was generally ineffective and that it destroyed many lives that could be useful to the revolution.[6] The attitude of the current leadership of the Soviet Union toward sub-state terrorism shows considerable continuity with the ideas of Lenin and Trotsky. The Soviets have supported a number of guerrilla movements in recent decades, including the movements in the former Portuguese colonies of Angola, Mozambique, and Guinea-Bissau; the pro-communist movements in Indochina; and the Greek communist guerrillas during the civil war in Greece after World War II. They are currently supporting guerrilla movements in Zimbabwe (Rhodesia) and in Namibia (Southwest Africa). However, on a number of occasions the Soviets have condemned certain of the more spectacular and indiscriminate acts of terrorism committed by militant revolutionary movements in the contemporary world. *Pravda* condemned the killing of one Belgian and two U.S. diplomats in Khartoum by

Black September terrorists.[7] The Soviet press indirectly criticized the incident at Ma'alot by reporting that "world public opinion" condemned the killing of Israeli children by Arab *fedayeen*.[8]

At the time of a visit by Yasser Arafat to Moscow in July and August of 1974 *Izvestia* published a sharp critique of the tactics of the Black September Palestinian group. *Izvestia* claimed that actions by Black September such as plane hijackings, letter bombs, and the killing of Israeli athletes at the Munich Olympics were doing great harm to the reputation of the Palestinian resistance movement.[9] And an article in the Soviet weekly *New Times* was sharply critical of the Italian Red Brigades for assassinating former Italian premier Aldo Moro. The *New Times* article criticized the Red Brigades as "pseudo-revolutionaries" lacking any real proletarian consciousness and claimed that their actions were of benefit only to those elements on the extreme right in Italy which would like to return to fascism.[10]

The Soviets have been particularly critical of George Habash, the leader of the Popular Front for the Liberation of Palestine (PFLP). The PFLP has carried out a number of spectacular acts of international terrorism. Perhaps the most famous was the series of hijackings in September 1970 in which a TWA 707, a Swissair DC-8, and a BOAC VC-10 were hijacked to Dawson airfield in northern Jordan while a Pan Am 747 was hijacked to Cairo. During Yasser Arafat's visit to Moscow in the summer of 1974, the Federation of Soviet Writers published an article which criticized Habash for "irresponsible acts" and "Maoist demagogism" and which claimed that his behavior was of benefit only to the enemies of the Palestinian people.[11]

Originally terrorism was defined in broad terms as one of several strategies whereby violence is used to effect social and political change. It is now appropriate to expand upon this definition by noting the specific tactical goals that a strategy of terrorism seeks to accomplish.

A major goal of many acts of terrorism carried out by various organizations is publicity. The terrorist group seeks to publicize its cause among two distinct audiences: first, the population in whose interests the group claims to be acting and second, the international community of nations or some portion of this community.

A number of examples can be cited of attempts to propagandize the first audience group. The following instances are typical:

A. In 1943 Nathan Yalin-Mor, one of the top leaders of Lehi (also known as the Stern group), wrote an article entitled "Kill, Get Killed, But Don't Get Arrested." In the article Yalin-Mor ordered Lehi members to always carry guns, and in the event they were asked by British police or soldiers for their identity cards, they were to pull out their guns and begin firing. The purpose of this tactic was to show that the members of Lehi had no respect for British authority in Palestine and that they were willing to die in defiance of what was to them an illegitimate authority. Yalin-Mor maintained that this evidence of willingness to sacrifice generated a great deal of favorable publicity for Lehi among the Jewish community in the Palestine mandate and had the additional benefit of intimidating those British responsible for identity checks.[12]

B. In his memoirs of the campaign in Cyprus against the British, General George Grivas noted how the targets and the assault techniques in a number of his early operations had been designed to alert the population of the island to the existence of a serious revolutionary movement.[13]

C. In an interview several years ago George Habash of the PFLP was asked about his tactic of staging spectacular acts of terrorism. In response to a question as to whether there would be further "spectaculars," Habash replied that there would be and that there must be. He went on to explain that such dramatic acts were essential if the PFLP were to achieve its goal of mobilizing the Palestinian people. He maintained that Palestine could be liberated only through a popular war waged by the Palestinian people.[14]

D. In October 1970 the Front de Libération du Quebec kidnapped James Cross, the British trade commissioner in Quebec province. The FLQ asked for the payment of a monetary ransom and the release of certain prisoners. The FLQ also demanded that its political manifesto be published on the front page of all of the principal newspapers in Quebec. Further, it demanded that this manifesto be read in full on Radio-Canada and its affiliated stations in Quebec province at some point during the prime time hours between 8 and 11 p.m.[15]

E. In January 1971 Sir Geoffrey Jackson, British ambassador to

Uruguay, was kidnapped by the Tupamaro guerrillas and held until the following September. During the course of his captivity Jackson had a number of conversations with his abductors as to their motivations in kidnapping him. He stated that one of their purposes was to conduct an act of what they called "armed propaganda." The Tupamaros felt that a spectacular act such as kidnapping and holding hostage an important figure like the British ambassador would alert the Uruguayan public to the power of their movement. It would show the public that the Tupamaros were in effect a "parallel government," that is, they could hold whomever they wanted to hostage in a "people's prison" for as long as they wanted, with the Uruguayan government being powerless to do anything about it.[16]

The second audience a terrorist group seeks to publicize its cause to is the international community as a whole or at least some portion of this community:

A. In 1944 Lord Moyne, British high commissioner for the Middle East, was assassinated by two members of Lehi. Nathan Yalin-Mor gave the following explanation for this assassination. Lord Moyne was responsible for enforcing the British ban on Jewish immigration to Palestine and for the repressive measures taken against the Jewish community there. But the world was unaware of British policies because of censorship. Lehi felt that a spectacular act such as the assassination of Moyne would focus world attention on the plight of the Jews under the British mandate in Palestine.[17]

B. In what he called a "preparatory general plan," which he apparently drew up two years before the beginning of his Cyprus campaign, General Grivas stated that the objective of his campaign would be to arouse international public opinion, especially among the allies of Greece, by dramatic terrorist acts. The British were to be harassed until they would be forced by international diplomacy exercised through the United Nations to agree to settle the Cyprus problem in accordance with "the desires of the Cypriot people and the whole Greek nation."[18]

C. In September 1970 George Habash's PFLP hijacked first two and then three airliners to Dawson field in northern Jordan. An attempt to hijack a fourth airliner, an El Al jet that had just taken off from London, failed with one of the two hijackers killed by El Al guards and the other taken into custody by the British authorities.

The second hijacker, Leila Khaled, was later set free as part of an exchange for the release of the captured crew and passengers. In her memoirs Khaled claimed that the September 1970 hijackings had forced the world to take notice of Palestine. She exultantly declared that "Palestine was on the lips of everyone the world over for a week."[19]

D. In January 1975 the Fraunces Tavern in New York City was bombed and four people were killed. The Fuerzas Armada de Liberación Nacional Puertorriquena (FALN), or Armed Forces for the National Liberation of Puerto Rico, claimed credit for the blast. *The New York Times* carried a feature story on the FALN a short time later in which José Alberto Alvarez, the first secretary of the American branch of the Puerto Rican Socialist party, said that the FALN might be using "drastic" methods to publicize the independence campaign. Alvarez noted that a United Nations resolution in favor of Puerto Rico's independence had received little attention in the press and stated that in contrast bomb explosions get big headlines and consequently many more people were aware of the Puerto Rican independence movement.[20]

A second goal of a terrorist campaign is to intimidate and harass authorities, to make life hard for them so as to force them to make concessions. The terrorist group seeks to deprive the opposition of something it values: material resources, law and order, or just simply peace of mind. In seeking this second goal the terrorists are engaging in a strategy of "coercive diplomacy":[21]

A. Nathan Yalin-Mor of Lehi summarized the strategy of his organization: "Our aim was to disrupt the British state organization in Palestine and to make life unbearable for them." He noted that to this end Lehi unleashed a series of attacks on telegraph centers, oil storage areas, military and police headquarters, and prisons. Roads were mined, and patrols of soldiers and police were ambushed.[22]

B. Another group in the Zionist Undergound in Palestine, the Irgun Zvai Leumi, had certain tactical disagreements with Lehi but likewise sought to harass the British. Eli Tavin, a former member of the high command of the Irgun, stated that they were waging a "war of nerves" against the British: life was made intolerable for the British by assassinations, by constant phoned-in bomb threats, by the public flogging of British officers, and by the hanging of two British noncommissioned officers in response to the execution of Irgun members.[23] Menachem Begin, then leader of the Irgun, graphically described this "war of nerves":

The forces of oppression knew no respite by day or by night. It was bad for them when operations were in progress; it was not good for them when there were no operations—for then they waited expectantly for some surprise "visit." Their nervous system might be compared to a broken down piano: you press one note and the whole piano emits a cacophony of noise. We did not have to attack twenty British camps simultaneously in order to develop acute apprehension amongst all. It was enough to attack one in order that all should be affected with fear by night and with uneasy expectation by day.[24]

Begin was aware that the actions of his organization were depriving the British of other valued commodities besides peace of mind, namely, money and manpower. He noted that Churchill made a speech in the House of Commons in March 1947 denouncing the Labor government for tying down 100,000 British troops in Palestine at a cost of 30 to 40 million pounds a year.[25]

C. In an interview in 1970 with a leader of the Popular Democratic Front for the Liberation of Palestine (PDFLP), an offshoot of George Habash's PFLP, the interviewer asked a question concerning the purposes of Palestinian attacks on Israeli targets. The PDFLP leader replied that one of the main goals of such attacks was to create as much disturbance and dislocation as possible in Israel, so as to prove to the Israelis that Zionism was no longer a comfortable or a viable option for them.[26]

D. In an interview in 1971 "Urbano," a code name for a leader of the Tupamaro guerrillas in Uruguay, stated that a number of the actions undertaken by the Tupamaros were designed to undermine the will to resist of the security forces of the regime. Urbano claimed that an increasingly large number of the members of the security forces had been demoralized by the Tupamaros and were beginning to question why they were defending the government.[27]

E. In an interview in October 1976 a high-ranking member of the Belfast branch of the Provisional Sinn Fein said that the Provisional IRA is seeking to make staying in Ulster expensive for Great Britain by disrupting the economy of the province and thereby forcing the British to pour in large subsidies to prevent total economic collapse.[28]

A third goal of many terrorist campaigns is to force the polarization of society. Terrorist groups pursuing this goal assume that if society can be polarized for and against the status quo, then the anti-status quo forces will be sufficiently powerful to bring down the regime. In working to divide a society, the particular terrorist organization has two audience groups: the population as a whole, which the revolutionary movement hopes will be forced by terroristic acts to choose sides, and the government, which the terrorists hope will respond to their acts with increased repression, thereby polarizing the situation.

Pierre Kropotkin, the Russian anarchist who lived from 1842 to 1921, is one example of a revolutionary who believed that terrorist acts would force the citizenry to choose sides for or against the incumbent regime. He wrote that indifference following acts of terrorism is impossible. People are forced to take notice of the terrorists and of their causes and to take sides for and against. An act of terrorism, he claimed, does more propagandizing than thousands of pamphlets.[29] The Tupamaros in Uruguay also believed that terrorism could force people to choose between the status quo and the cause of the revolutionaries. In an interview in 1970 a Tupamaro leader stated that once an urban terrorist campaign·was launched all of forces on the left would be mobilized into a united front of opposition to the incumbent government.[30]

The second audience group involved in any attempt to polarize society is, as mentioned above, the government. The following are instances of terrorist groups seeking to force the polarization of society by making the government more repressive.

A. Sir Geoffrey Jackson stated that in talking to his captors it became clear that one of the reasons he had been kidnapped was to force the Uruguayan government to be more repressive. The Tupamaros apparently hoped that the spectacle of their being able to abduct and hold prisoner the ambassador of an important country would goad the government into repressive acts.[31]

B. Sean Holly, the American labor attaché in Guatemala who was kidnapped in 1970, stated that his kidnappers told him that they believed repression would speed up the revolution, and thus they sought to incite repression by acts such as kidnapping.[32]

C. The Brazilian theorist of urban guerrilla warfare Carlos Marighella advocated provoking governmental repression in his "Minimanual of the Urban Guerrilla." He stated that governmental repressive measures such as mass arrests, house searches, closing off
streets, and political assassinations would make life increasingly
unbearable for the population. The people would blame the government for the disruption of their lives and would swing their
support behind the urban guerrillas.[33]

D. In 1970 and 1971, as it was building up for its current campaign to drive the British out of Northern Ireland, the Provisional
IRA launched calculated provocations of the British army so as to
cause repressive measures to be taken against the Catholic population of Ulster. The Provisional IRA felt that such repressive measures would alienate the Catholic population from the British and
give the IRA a mass base of popular support.[34]

A fourth goal of terrorist acts is to aggravate relations between
states so as to prevent a set of political events unfavorable to the
terrorist group. For example, in 1918 the Russian Social Revolutionaries assassinated the German ambassador in Moscow and the
German governor general in the occupied Ukraine in the hope of
sabotaging the peace settlement that had been reached between
Lenin's Bolsheviks and the German government.[35] In more recent
times a number of the most spectacular terrorist acts of the Palestinian movement have been undertaken with the objective of worsen-
ing relations between Israel and the Arab states. The Palestinians
have long been fearful that the Arab governments might at some
point seek to come to terms with Israel at their expense and consequently have staged a number of major terrorist incidents with the
hope that these incidents would prevent any Arab-Israeli accom-
modation:

A. One of the motivations of the September 1970 hijackings of
three aircraft to Jordan by the PFLP was to sabotage the Rogers
peace initiative in the Middle East.[36]

B. In December 1973 a group of Palestinian *fedayeen* machine-
gunned passengers and fire-bombed a parked airliner at the Rome
airport, killing thirty-two people. The terrorists then seized another
airliner and flew to Kuwait. The *fedayeen* were apparently trying
to raise tensions in the Middle East in the hope of sabotaging the
Geneva peace conference.[37]

C. In May 1974 a group of eighty-five Israeli schoolchildren were seized by three members of the PDFLP at Ma'alot. Negotiations between the Israelis and the PDFLP broke down, and the building where the children were being held was stormed. Some twenty-six children were killed in the assault. Naif Hawatme, the leader of the PDFLP, called a press conference after the incident in which he stated that the purpose of the attack had been to defeat Henry Kissinger's peace drive and to destroy any solution that would leave Israel still exisitng.[38]

The fifth goal of terrorist action is the freeing of prisoners and the securing of monetary ransoms. In Guatemala in March 1970 the Fuerzas Armadas Rebeldes (FAR) kidnapped the German ambassador to Guatemala, Count Karl von Spreti. The FAR demanded the release of twenty-five prisoners and the payment of $700,000 in ransom. The Guatemalan government refused, and von Spreti was killed.[39] In July and August of 1970 there were three political kidnappings in Uruguay by the Tupamaros: Daniel Mitrione, an Agency for International Development adviser to the Uruguayan police; Aloisio Mares Dias Gomide, a Brazilian Consul; and Claude Fly, an American agricultural adviser. The Tupamaros demanded the release of 150 prisoners. When the Uruguayan government refused this demand, the Tupamaros killed Mitrione. Fly and Dias Gomide were held for a period of several months and then released.[40] In the October 1970 kidnappings in Quebec the FLQ demanded the release of thirteen prisoners and the payment of $500,000 in gold in return for the release of kidnapped British diplomat James Cross. The FLQ got neither demand; however, in exchange for releasing Cross unharmed, the FLQ members responsible were flown to Cuba.[41] While seizing hostages to get prisoners released or to secure ransoms is, generally speaking, a new tactic for revolutionary movements, the problems which give rise to this tactic have been recurrent among such movements. Revolutionary movements have always faced the twin problems of how to provide the movement with the necessary funds and how to free captured comrades. Revolutionary leaders have resorted to a variety of responses to these problems. Lenin, for example, authorized bank robberies to secure funds for the Bolshevik movement.[42] Menachem Begin organized a daring assault on the British prison at Acre to free captured members of the Irgun.[43]

* * *

There is as well the issue of the morality of terrorism, which is especially relevant since terrorists usually attempt to justify their actions. And it is difficult to analyze terrorism unless the moral rationales that terrorists offer for their actions are considered.

The wave of terrorist incidents in recent years has produced a great deal of criticism of terrorist tactics. Such criticism should be approached cautiously because virtually all commentators on terrorism approach the problem with biases and self-serving interests. For example, the strong criticisms of terrorism that come from governments such as those of Rhodesia, South Africa, and Brazil are to be regarded as rather suspect. These governments are no strangers to indiscriminate violence; their real reason for opposing terrorism is that they oppose social change in general, whether violent or or nonviolent.

But there also have been a number of condemnations of terrorism from individuals against whom the charge of having a double standard is less credible. In particular, one might note two articles on the morality of terrorism by Michael Walzer and Irving Howe that came out in the summer of 1975. Walzer and Howe are members of the socialist left and hence cannot be dismissed as opposing terrorism because they oppose all social change. Both authors made the same argument: that while certain limited forms of violence can be justified, indiscriminate terrorism is morally wrong. Walzer argued that while there is a moral rationale for the assassination of leaders who act in Hitlerian ways, this rationale does not justify the current wave of terrorist acts. The assassin of a despot, he maintained, fights a limited war and discriminates in his choice of targets. The current generation of terrorists, on the other hand, wage total and indiscriminate war against nations, ethnic groups, and religions.[44] Howe argued that for tyrannicide to clearly be morally justifiable there must be an appreciable difference between the tyrant and his likely successor. He stated that killing a Stalin was morally defensible because such an assassination would mean the removal of a dictator whose taste for blood went far beyond the level of repressiveness necessary to keep him in power. However, killing a Brezhnev was much less justifiable, because Brezhnev would undoubtedly be replaced by another quite similar Soviet bureaucrat.[45]

In other words, Howe and Walzer are arguing that the sort of terrorism that makes no distinction between guilty and innocent or between combatant and noncombatant is morally unjustifiable. It should be stressed that a number of the practitioners of terrorism have agreed with them. This point is especially important to remember in light of the popular stereotype of the terrorist as a deranged individual who kills out of a psychopathic lust for violence. The following quotations from prominent twentieth-century revolutionaries on the immorality of nonselective terrorism are worth quoting at length.

Michael Collins (chief of staff of the IRA during the Black and Tan War; assassinated in 1922 during the Irish civil war):
  We struck at individuals, and by so doing we cut their lines of communication; and we shook their morale. And we conducted the conflict . . . as far as possible, according to the rules of war. Only the armed forces and the spies and criminal agents of the British government were attacked.[46]

Menachem Begin (commander of the Irgun Zvai Leumi):

. . . I emphasized that the employment of explosives would be distinguished by a new device. . . . On the one hand our "mines" could not be moved or dismantled as they would blow up on contact. On the other hand we would be able to fix the moment for the explosion of these "mines" by a time mechanism, half-an-hour or even an hour before their introduction into the building. This would allow for evacuation by hotel guests, workers and officials. The rules we laid down for ourselves made the evacuation of the [King David] hotel essential. There were many civilians in the hotel whom we wanted, at all costs, to avoid injuring. We were anxious to insure that they should leave the danger zone in plenty of time for their safety.[47]

Sean MacBride (chief of staff of the IRA and Nobel Peace Prize laureate):

It used to be the rule, always, that you had to take precautions not to injure innocents or civilians. In any actions we took, ambushes or military actions, it was always the rule that we had to protect people from the effects of our battles. Very often, areas were cleared beforehand.[48]

General George Grivas (commander of EOKA):

EOKA harmed only those who harmed us; I never ordered an attack on a woman or child throughout the struggle and anything of that sort would have been severely punished. I ordered the release of John Cremer, the Englishman who was taken hostage in August 1956, when I learned he was an elderly man. The British made atrocity propaganda out of the death of a government official and his wife who were shot while driving in the Kyrenian mountains; this would not have occurred if the man had not first drawn a gun and fired.[49]

However, while it is important to recognize that many terrorists have not believed in indiscriminate violence, it is equally true that many of the current terrorist groups do kill indiscriminately. Yet these groups are not amoral in the sense that they offer no justifications for their actions. On the contrary, there are several arguments offered as moral rationales for their attacks.

The first and simplest argument is to deny that the violence was indiscriminate, that is, to deny that the victims were innocent people. Often the terrorist greatly narrows the definition of innocent people. In February 1970 the Popular Front for the Liberation of Palestine—General Command (PFLP-GC), a splinter of George Habash's PFLP, blew up an Israel-bound Swiss airplane in flight, killing all forty-seven passengers and crew. The PFLP-GC justified its attack by saying that the eleven Israelis on board were not innocent victims but instead were high government officials.[50] In the course of an interview with Oriana Fallaci, George Habash stated that non-Israeli tourists to Israel were not innocent bystanders because they had failed to ask permission to go to Israel from the legitimate owners of the country, namely, the Palestinians.[51] In some instances this process of narrowing down the definition of indiscriminate violence goes to a point where it is proclaimed that no one is innocent—that everyone shares in the responsibility for society's wrongs. Emile Henry, a nineteenth-century French anarchist who bombed a crowded Paris café, killing one person and injuring twenty others, stated at his trial that his only regret was that he had not killed more people. "But those were innocent people you struck," exclaimed one of his judges. "There are no innocent people," replied Henry.[52] Similarly, Sir Geoffrey Jackson reported that a number of his Tupamaro captors stated flatly, "There is no such thing as an innocent bystander."[53]

A second argument is that national liberation struggles, like every form of war, involve casualties among civilians. The British journalist Christopher Dobson in his book *Black September* quotes an al Fatah official as saying, "How else can we bring pressure to bear on the world? The deaths are regrettable, but they are a fact of war in which innocents become involved."[54] In early 1976, as fighting raged in Angola between the Frente Nacional de Libertação de Angola (FNLA, or National Front for the Liberation of Angola) and the Movimento Popular para a Libertação de Angola (MPLA, or Popular Movement for the Liberation of Angola), the foreign minister of the FNLA, Paulo Tuba, called a press conference in which he threatened acts of international terrorism against those nations backing the MPLA. When asked about the civilian victims of such a campaign of terrorism, he replied: "In a war of national liberation people have to die. This is a fundamental principle of a war of liberation. These are necessary sacrifices."[55] And in justifying Lod Airport incident al Fatah made the following comments: "All Palestine is under occupation and we have the right to fight so as to eliminate this occupation. If the fighting hits civilians, then this is in the nature of war from which nobody escapes."[56]

A third justification is that the groups of people whom the terrorists claim to speak for have suffered greatly and, therefore, if other people have to suffer that is a tragic but unavoidable consequence of efforts to rectify a serious wrong. In response to the widespread condemnation of its attack at Lod Airport the PFLP claimed that the Israelis had no right to complain about the deaths at Lod Airport because that was the site of a 1948 Israeli massacre of a number of Arab women, children, and old people.[57] After the Ma'alot incident a Beirut newspaper quoted a Palestinian leader to the effect that the real crime was not the deaths at Ma'alot but rather the destruction twenty-six years earlier of the Arab village of Tarshila and the expulsion of the village's population so as to make way for the Israeli settlement of Ma'alot. This Palestinian leader went on to say that the Western news media were ignoring the savage Israeli bombing raids on the refugee camps, raids in which many Palestinian children were being killed.[58] Leila Khaled, in her memoirs of her service with the PFLP, voiced quite emphatically the idea that the suffering of the Palestinian people justified violence against other people. Khaled recalled how, as she was preparing to hijack a TWA airliner in 1969, she began to worry that some of the children on board the plane might be killed or wounded in the hijacking. She stated that she resolved her doubts by remembering that the children of her own people had suffered enormously and were looking to her for help in their plight.[59]

The fourth justification is that the government authorities are the real ones responsible for the violence. This argument has two variations. The first is that in hostage situations any fatalities are the government's fault because it refused to make the necessary concessions. After the Munich incident a Palestinian radio station operating out of Cairo made the following statement: "The real murderer is the arrogance of the Zionist enemy, who insisted on not complying with the *fedayeen's* humane demand."[60] During the Quebec crisis in the fall of 1970 the FLQ leaders put out a communiqué in which they maintained that they were quite willing to execute their kidnap victim James Cross. They went on to state, "The present authorities alone will be truly responsible for his death."[61] In an interview a short while after the death of Daniel Mitrione in August 1970, a Tupamaro leader stated that Mitrione had been allowed to die by President Pacheco of Uruguay and by the American Embassy because they thought that Mitrione's death would be a setback for the Tupamaros.[62]

The second variation of the argument that the party really responsible for indiscriminate terror is the government is that the authorities will not allow peaceful change, and hence the only means for change is through violence. The final declaration of the conference in Havana in 1966 of representatives from various Asian, African, and Latin American revolutionary movements claimed that every step toward freedom and independence had been won by armed struggle and that there are no instances in which the exploiters repented and voluntarily agreed to allow peaceful progress.[63] The Ejército Revolucionario del Peublo— People's Revolutionary Army (ERP)—in Argentina put out a communiqué in which it stated that national and social liberation could not be accomplished through elections. "Power," the communiqué stated, "is not born from votes. Power is born from gun-point."[64] In separate interviews in September 1976 with Joe Cahill, vice-president of the Provisional Sinn Fein, and with Sean Keenan, editor of the Provisional's newspaper *An Phoblacht*, the ongoing campaign of the Provisional IRA to drive the British out of Northern Ireland was justified by the argument that British intransigence made peaceful and constitutional efforts to unify Ireland impossible. Both individuals claimed that the history of British-Irish relations showed that Irish freedom from British imperialism could be won only by physical force.[65]

The fifth justification is that the opposition practices indiscriminate violence and, hence, by implication, acts of terrorism are justified in response to such violence. Emma Goldman, a well-known American anarchist of the early decades of the twentieth century, stated that "compared with the wholesale violence of capital and government, political acts of violence are but a drop in the ocean."[66] In his speech at the United Nations in November 1974 Yasser Arafat denounced the state of Israel for practicing terrorism. He stated that the shooting down of a Libyan airliner in December 1972, the destruction of the Syrian city of Quneitra, and the bombing of refugee camps in southern Lebanon were all examples of Israeli terrorism.[67] Gerry Adams, former commander of the Belfast brigade of the IRA, accused the British of maintaining their control in Northern Ireland by allowing those who want Northern Ireland to remain part of the United Kingdom to engage in terrorism.[68]

NOTES

1. Walter Laqueur, *Terrorism* (Boston: Little, Brown & Company, 1977), pp. 63-65.

2. V. I. Lenin, "Why the Social Democrats Must Declare Determined and Relentless War on the Socialist Revolutionaries" (1902) and "Where to Begin" (1901), in *Lenin Reader*, ed. Stefan Possony (Chicago: Henry Regnery Company, 1966), pp. 470-472.

3. V. I. Lenin, "What Is to Be Done?" in *Lenin on Politics and Revolution*, ed. James Connor (New York: Pegasus Press, 1968), pp. 51-52.

4. Leon Trotsky, "The Marxist Position on Individual Terrorism," in

Leon Trotsky: Against Individual Terrorism, ed. Will Reissner (New York: Pathfinder Press, 1974), pp. 6-7.

5. Leon Trotsky, "The Bankruptcy of Terrorism," in *Leon Trotsky: Against Individual Terrorism*, pp. 13-14.

6. Ché Guevera, *Guerrilla Warfare* (New York: Bantam Books, 1968), pp. 15-16.

7. Roger O. Freedman, "Soviet Policy Toward International Terrorism," in *International Terrorism*, ed. Yonah Alexander (New York: AMS Press, 1976), p. 133.

8. Interview No. 1 (Galia Golan).

9. Levi Tolokonov, *Izvestia*, July 31, 1974, quoted in *Journal of Palestine Studies*, Vol. IV, No. 1 (Autumn 1974), p. 175.

10. Vadim Ardatovsky, "Of Those Who Kidnapped Aldo Moro," *Soviet Press* (Washington, D.C.: Bolling Air Force Base, July 1978), pp. 208-209.

11. *The Journal of Palestine Studies*, Vol. IV, No. 1 (Autumn 1974), pp. 168-169.

12. Interview No. 7 (Nathan Yalin-Mor). This tactic was very controversial. Menachem Begin claimed that it got a lot of people killed for no good reason. See Menachem Begin, *The Revolt* (Jerusalem: Steimatzky's Agency Limited, 1972), pp. 106-108.

13. George Grivas, *The Memoirs of General Grivas* (New York: Frederick A. Praeger, 1965), p. 31.

14. Christopher Dobson, *Black September* (New York: The Macmillan Company, 1974), p. 62.

15. John Saywell, *Quebec 70* (Toronto: University of Toronto Press, 1970), p. 35.

16. Interview No. 9 (Sir Geoffrey Jackson). The idea of acts of "armed propaganda" among contemporary revolutionaries bears a strong resemblance to the concept of nineteenth-century revolutionaries of the "propaganda of the deed."

17. Interview No. 7 (Nathan Yalin-Mor).

18. Grivas, *Memoirs*, p. 204.

19. Leila Khaled, *My People Shall Live* (London: Hodden and Staughton, 1973), p. 214.

20. *New York Times*, February 7, 1975.

21. Thomas C. Schelling, *Arms and Influence* (New Haven: Yale University Press, 1966), passim.

22. Interview No. 7 (Nathan Yalin-Mor).

23. Interview No. 8 (Eli Tavin).

24. Begin, *The Revolt*, p. 322.

25. Ibid., pp. 318 and 322.

26. "Interview with Top-Ranking PDFLP Member," in *Towards Revolu-*

tion, Vol. I, ed. John Gerassi (London: Weidenfeld and Nicolson, 1971), p. 236.

27. "Interview with 'Urbano' by Leopoldo Madruga," in *Urban Guerrilla Warfare in Latin America*, ed. James Kohl and John Litt (Cambridge, Massachusetts: The M.I.T. Press, 1974), p. 281.

28. Interview No. 13 (Belfast member of Provisional Sinn Fein).

29. Pierre Kropotkin, *Paroles d'un Revolté* (Paris: C. Marpon and E. Flammarion, undated), p. 286.

30. "Thirty Answers to Thirty Questions, Clandestine Interview with Unidentified Tupamaro Leader," *Towards Revolution*, Vol. II, p. 248.

31. Interview No. 9 (Sir Geoffrey Jackson).

32. Interview No. 33 (Sean Holly).

33. Carlos Marighella, "The Minimanual of the Urban Guerrilla," appendix in Robert Moss, *Urban Guerrilla Warfare* (London: International Institute for Strategic Studies, 1971), p. 40.

34. J. Bowyer Bell, "Strategy, Tactics, and Terror: An Irish Perspective," in *International Terrorism*, pp. 71-73.

35. Laqueur, *Terrorism*, p. 81.

36. William B. Quandt, Fuad Jabber, and Ann Mosely Lesch, *The Politics of Palestinian Nationalism* (Berkeley, California: University of California Press, 1973), p. 125.

37. *New York Times*, December 18, 1973.

38. Edward Weisband and Damir Roguly, "Palestinian Terrorism: Violence, Verbal Strategy, and Legitimacy," in *International Terrorism*, pp. 304-305.

39. Brian M. Jenkins and Janera Johnson, *International Terrorism: A Chronology, 1968-1974* (Santa Monica, California: The RAND Corporation, R-1597-DOS/ARPA, 1975), p. 23.

40. Ibid., p. 20.

41. Ibid., p. 25.

42. For a description of several of these robberies, see David Shub, *Lenin* (New York: Doubleday & Company, Inc., 1948), p. 98.

43. Begin, *The Revolt*, pp. 275-290.

44. Michael Walzer, "The New Terrorists," *The New Republic*, Vol. 173, No. 9 (August 30, 1975), p. 13.

45. Irving Howe, "The Return of Terror," *Dissent*, Vol. 22, No. 3 (Summer 1975), p. 229.

46. "Terrorism," *Skeptic*, No. 11 (January/February 1976), p. 11.

47. Begin, *The Revolt*, pp. 212-213.

48. "Interview with Sean MacBride," *Skeptic*, No. 11 (January/February 1976), p. 11.

49. Grivas, *Memoirs*, p. 169n.

50. Weisband and Roguly, "Palestinian Terrorism," p. 284.

51. Dobson, *Black September*, p. 31.

52. "Terrorism," *Skeptic*, No. 11 (January/February 1976), p. 37.

53. Interview No. 9 (Sir Geoffrey Jackson).

54. Dobson, *Black September*, pp. 54-55.

55. *New York Times*, January 15, 1976.

56. Cairo MENA in Arabic, May 31, 1972. Department of Commerce, National Technical Information Service: Foreign Broadcast Information Service. Middle East and North Africa, June 1, 1972, p. A1.

57. Baghdad INA in Arabic, June 5, 1972. Department of Commerce, National Technical Information Service: Foreign Broadcast Information Service. Middle East and North Africa, June 5, 1972, p. A1.

58. Mahmoud Dorwish, "Anti-Arab Prejudice in Europe," *Al-Muharris* (Beirut Newspaper), quoted in *Journal of Palestine Studies*, Vol. III, No. 4 (Summer 1974), p. 166.

59. Khaled, *My People*, p. 133.

60. Cairo Voice of Palestine in Arabic to Arab World, September 6, 1972. Department of Commerce, National Technical Information Service: Foreign Broadcast Information Service. Middle East and North Africa, September 7, 1972, p. A1.

61. Saywell, *Quebec 70*, p. 39.

62. "Interview with 'Urbano' by Leopoldo Madruga," in *Urban Guerrilla Warfare in Latin America*, p. 270.

63. "A War to the Finish," Declaration of the Tricontinental Organization of Solidarity of the Peoples of Africa, Asia, and Latin America (OSPAAAL), in *Towards Revolution*, Vol. II, pp. 753-754.

64. J. Bowyer Bell, *Transnational Terror* (Washington, D.C.: American Enterprise Institute, 1975), p. 53.

65. Interviews No. 11 (Joe Cahill) and No. 12 (Sean Keenan).

66. Emma Goldman, "The Psychology of Political Violence," in *The Terrorism Reader*, ed. Walter Laqueur (New York: Meridian, 1978), p. 197.

67. "Yasser Arafat's Speech to the U.N.," *Journal of Palestine Studies*, Vol. IV, No. 2 (Winter 1975), p. 189.

68. Gerry Adams, *Peace in Ireland?* (Belfast, Northern Ireland: The Belfast Republican Press Centre, 1976), p. 8.

chapter 4

TERRORISM AND
INTERNATIONAL POLITICS

International terrorist groups have contributed in several respects to aggravating relations between the states making up the international system. One way in which terrorist groups contribute to the aggravation of relations between nations concerns situations where a diplomat from country A is kidnapped while serving in country B. The terrorists holding the diplomat demand the release of prisoners and/or the payment of a ransom from B's government. If country B refuses, then country A will often be angered and relations between the two countries will suffer.

On March 31, 1970, the West German ambassador to Guatemala, Count Karl von Spreti, was kidnapped by the FAR, a Guatemalan guerrilla group. The FAR demanded the release of twenty-five prisoners and the payment of a $700,000 ransom. The Guatemalan government refused the demands, and the ambassador was killed. The West German government, angered by the Guatemalan refusal to meet the demands, protested vigorously and reduced diplomatic contacts with Guatemala to a minimum. The West German acting chief of mission and most of his aides were recalled. The Guatemalan ambassador in Bonn was asked to leave the country.[1] On July 31, 1970, the Tupamaro guerrillas kidnapped Aloisio Mares Dias Gomide, a Brazilian consul. They demanded the release of 150 prisoners being held by the Uruguayan government. When the Uruguayans refused to make concessions or to negotiate with the

Tupamaros, the Brazilian authorities were angered and filed protests with the Uruguayan government. Dias Gomide was finally
released in February 1971 after his wife raised a $250,000 ransom.[2]

A second way that terrorists can aggravate state-to-state relations
occurs when a national of state A is seized on the territory of state B.
If the government of state A feels that the government of state B is
not handling the negotiations properly, then at times state A will
bypass the authorities in state B and negotiate directly with the
terrorists. Because governments as a rule do not like other nations
bargaining with their domestic insurgents, the result is often a
deterioration of relations. Some examples follow.

A. In early 1974 Françoise Claustre, a French archaeologist, was
abducted by insurgents in northern Chad. There followed a prolonged process of negotiation and bargaining. At first the French
government agreed to let the authorities in Chad handle the negotiations. But in the spring of 1975, impatient with the length of the
negotiations and convinced that Chad had no intention of making
the sort of concessions necessary to free Claustre, the French initiated
their own contacts with the rebels. The guerrillas demanded the
payment of a ransom of $2,200,000 in supplies and cash. The
French agreed to pay. In October 1975 the French began to air-drop
the money and the supplies to the insurgents. The government of
Chad, furious at being bypassed and at having its domestic opposition supplied by the French, ousted a French expeditionary force of
some 2,000 personnel that had been fighting the rebels in Chad.[3]

B. In May 1975 one Dutch and three American students were
kidnapped while doing anthropological research in Tanzania. The
four students were taken from Tanzania into Zaire. Their abductors were part of a guerrilla movement in Zaire. The guerrillas
demanded arms and a cash ransom in return for the release of the
students.

The American ambassador to Tanzania, Beverly Carter, initiated
contact with the rebels in Zaire. He arranged to have the ransom
money that the parents of the students had raised sent to the guerrillas. The insurgents released the students in June 1975. The government of Zaire was intensely angered by the actions of Ambassador
Carter and communicated its anger to Washington. The Zaire
authorities were so resentful of Carter's actions that at one point

during the negotiations a boat on Lake Tanganyika containing several American officials seeking to establish contact with the rebels was fired on by a gunboat from Zaire.[4]

A third way in which acts of transnational terrorism can worsen relations between nations is when a nation refuses to punish the perpetrators of an act of terrorism carried out on its soil against a national of another state:

A. At the Munich Olympics in September 1972 an eight-man Black September squad killed two members of the Israeli team and captured nine more. The West German authorities decided to use force in an attempt to free the hostages, but their attempt miscarried. All nine of the hostages and five of the terrorists were killed in a shootout at the Munich airport.

On October 29, 1972, a Lufthansa 727 was hijacked by members of Black September. The terrorists threatened to blow up the plane unless their compatriots in Munich were released. The West Germans complied with the terrorists' demand. The three Black September survivors were flown from Munich to Zagreb, Yugoslavia, and then on to Tripoli, Libya.[5]

The Israeli government was very bitter at the West German authorities. Israel protested "with all urgency and gravity" the West German decision to release the terrorists.[6] The Histadrut, the Israeli labor federation, stated that it would "end all visits by trade unionists and workers to Germany in a sign of protest against the freeing of those behind the killing in Munich."[7]

B. In November 1971 Wasfi el-Tal, the prime minister of Jordan, was assassinated in Cairo by members of Black September. The four assassins were tried but were never convicted because of the pressure on President Anwar Sadat from various sources in the Arab world, in particular Muammar el-Khaddafi of Libya. Jordan's King Hussein, angered by Sadat's refusal to punish el-Tal's assassins, halted efforts that were then under way to patch up Egyptian-Jordanian relations.[8]

Situations in which terrorists use the territory of state A as a base for operations against state B without the authorization of state A are a fourth source of terrorist-induced friction between states.

A. On August 15, 1974, an assassin attempted to kill President Park Chung Hee of South Korea. The attempt failed, but one of the assassin's bullets killed Park's wife. Prior to his attempt on Park's life, the assassin had been living among the large Korean community in Japan, where he had been recruited by anti-Park Koreans. Two weeks after the assassination attempt, Park summoned the Japanese ambassador and demanded a crackdown on the anti-Park groups in Japan. When the Japanese government replied that it would do nothing to harass opposition groups that were legal in Japan, relations between South Korea and Japan worsened.[9]

B. In the Basque region of Spain there have been a number of terrorist incidents in recent years by Basque separatists. The Basque insurgents have several bases in the Basque areas of France. As a result France's relations with Spain have been worsened in the past few years by the French refusal to liquidate these bases.[10]

The fifth complication that terrorist groups introduce into state-to-state relations is due to the migration of populations. In cases where the nationals of state A, having gone to work or study in state B, begin to undertake terrorist operations against a state C, the result frequently will be a crackdown by state B. State A will then be angered at the repression of its nationals. After the death of the eleven Israeli athletes at the Munich Olympics, the West Germans, angered because the Arab workers and students in West Germany were giving support to the Palestinian terrorists, instituted stern repressive measures toward Arab workers and student organizations in the FRG. The Arab states, in particular Egypt, lodged protests against these measures.[11]

* * *

In the above instances terrorist groups were able to aggravate relations between countries that had at least normal (if not friendly) relations with each other. In cases where a pair or group of nations have tense relations, terrorist groups have the potential to seriously escalate tensions, perhaps even to the point of war.

The outbreak of hostilities between Serbia and Austria-Hungary in 1914 that led to World War I originated with the assassination in Sarajevo of Archduke Franz Ferdinand and his wife on June 28, 1914. The assassination was the work of a secret Serbian terrorist group called Union or Death (also known as the Black Hand). This group was formed in 1911 with the aim of uniting Croatia, Slovenia, and Bosnia-Herzegovina with Serbia to form a "Greater Serbia."[12] Although the Black Hand included many high Serbian government and military officials, there is no evidence that Premier Nikola Pashitch of Serbia and his cabinet had anything to do with originating the assassination plot.[13] But the Austro-Hungarian government, already deeply concerned about the danger that Serbian nationalism was posing to their empire, decided that drastic action was necessary to eliminate this danger once and for all. So Austria-Hungary made a set of impossible demands on Serbia and then declared war when Serbia made an unsatisfactory response.[14] A. J. P. Taylor in *The Struggle for Mastery in Europe, 1848-1918* stated with reference to the outbreak of World War I: "The Austro-Hungarian declaration of war on Serbia was the decisive act; everything else followed from it."[15]

Due to Serbian claims on Austro-Hungarian territory, the relations between the two states had been tense for a number of years before the Sarajevo incident.[16] The incident must be seen in the context of this already existing friction so as to not be overemphasized in importance. But what the assassinations did do was to escalate the tensions between Serbia and Austria-Hungary, and hence between the Dual Alliance and the Triple Entente, to the level of war. In his study of the origins of World War I Sidney Fay argued that the effect of the assassinations at Sarajevo was to consolidate all the elements of international hostility such as economic rivalry and armaments races that had characterized the decades prior to World War I and to set in motion the succession of events that led to the outbreak of war.[17]

The relationship between Israel and its Arab neighbors provides a second example of how terrorists can help escalate tensions to the level of war. The 1956 and 1967 Middle Eastern wars had many differences, but both were similar in that they were in large part the outgrowth of a pattern of escalation in which raids by Palestinian terrorists played a major role. The process of escalation in both wars essentially involved three stages.

In the first stage there were raids against Israel by Palestinians, and the Israelis responded with reprisals. In mid-February 1955, a *fedayeen* raiding party penetrated deep into Israel, reaching the outskirts of Tel Aviv. The party did some damage and then returned to Egypt. David Ben-Gurion, newly restored to power after a couple of years in semiretirement, was determined to try to teach the Arabs a lesson. On February 28, 1955, the Israelis launched a major attack on the Egyptian military headquarters in Gaza. The raid inflicted heavy casualties on the Egyptians and severely damaged a number of installations.[18] Similarly, in 1966 the Israeli army conducted a major raid against the town of Samu in Jordan in retaliation for a series of raids that al Fatah had made from Jordanian territory.[19]

In the second stage of escalation, the nation that was the direct or indirect target of the reprisal, feeling humiliated by the reprisal, becomes even more belligerent toward the nation that launched the reprisal. In the case of the Gaza reprisal, there is substantial evidence that prior to the raid the Egyptians were taking what steps they could to keep the Palestinian guerrillas from making raids into Israel. Embittered and humiliated by the attack on their military headquarters, the Egyptians began forming *fedayeen* squads for raids into Israel. Dan Horowitz, an Israeli expert on his country's reprisal policy, stated that before the Gaza raid the Palestinian guerrillas acted against the wishes of the Egyptians but that after the raid the guerrillas received Egyptian aid.[20] Yair Evron agrees with Horowitz that the Egyptian decision to establish *fedayeen* units came after the Gaza raid.[21] Perhaps the most conclusive evidence that the Egyptian support of the *fedayeen* attacks against Israel began after the Gaza raid comes from Moshe Dayan's *Diary of the Sinai Campaign.* In this diary Dayan states that the Egyptian decision to set up *fedayeen* units was made in April 1955, that is, two months after the Gaza reprisal.[22]

In the case of the Samu reprisal, the immediate target was Jordan, but the effects of the reprisal were felt in other countries as well. Nasser in particular felt humiliated, because immediately after the attack the Jordanians unleased a propaganda offensive against him demanding to know why he had not come to their aid.[23] Nasser was concerned about the impact that this propaganda was having in the Arab world. Consequently, in May 1967, following the Syrian-

Israeli air battle in April over Damascus and the Soviet-inspired rumors of an Israeli invasion of Syria, he was quick to order his army into the Sinai to avoid another loss of prestige.[24]

In the third stage the actions taken by the recipients of the reprisals escalated an already tense situation into war. In 1956 the renewed raids of the *fedayeen* against Israel after the Israeli attack on Gaza were one of the three major causes of the Israeli invasion of Egypt (the other two being the closing of the Straits of Tiran and the Czech arms deal).[25] In 1967 the Egyptian decision to send a large military force into the Sinai was the step that set in motion the Israeli decision to preempt. The Jerusalem government perceived the Egyptian troop concentrations as a serious danger to the nation's security. It could not allow the Egyptians to remain in the Sinai. Nasser, however, had no intention of backing down: the mobilizing, the ousting of the United Nations buffer force, and the closing of the Strait of Tiran had won him an enormous propaganda victory in the Arab world. To have retreated would have invited the savage criticism that had followed his inactivity after Samu. The result was that the Israeli government, being unable to continue a costly mobilization indefinitely and feeling that all avenues for a diplomatic resolution of the crisis were exhausted, decided to attack.[26]

The present focus does not mean that terrorism was the sole or even the most important cause of the Middle Eastern wars of 1956 and 1967. There were a number of other causes: the widespread fear and hatred of Israel in the Arab world;[27] the rivalry among the Arab states that made the issue of Israel a political football and caused Arab states to try to appear to be the most vociferously anti-Israel; the flow of Soviet arms to its allies in the Middle East and of Western arms to Israel, which created a precarious military balance; and the narrow margin of error for the Israelis, who constantly felt the pressure to preempt because they could not afford to lose a war. Still the processes of escalation in 1955-1956 and in 1966-1967 document conclusively that the activities of terrorist groups were a significant factor in moving an already tense set of state-to-state relationships toward war.

* * *

International law is the area in which the third major impact of terrorism on the international system has been felt. The resurgence of terrorism in the last decade has set off two major controversies among international legal experts: (a) Is the instigation of terrorist acts by one state against another state illegal under international law? (b) What are the legal recourses available to a state that suffers from terrorist attacks?

Yehuda Z. Blum, a professor at the University of Tel Aviv School of Law, has argued that fomenting acts of terrorism by one state against another is a violation of international law.[28] Blum centers his argument around two United Nations documents, the 1951 Draft Code of Offenses Against the Peace and Security of Mankind (drawn up by the United Nations International Law Commission) and the 1965 Declaration of the Inadmissibility of Intervention in the Domestic Affairs of States and the Protection of Their Independence and Sovereignty (which was adopted by the General Assembly). The relevant passages follow:

Article 2(6) of the Draft Code of Offenses Against the Peace and Security of Mankind (this article was part of a list of crimes against peace and security):

The undertaking or encouragement by the authorities of a State of terrorist activities in another State, or the toleration by the authorities of a State of organized activities calculated to carry out terrorist acts in another state.[29]

Article 2 of the Declaration of the Inadmissibility of Intervention in the Domestic Affairs of States and the Protection of Their Independence and Sovereignty:

. . . no State shall organize, assist, foment, finance, invite or tolerate subversive, terrorist or armed activities directed towards the violent overthrow of the regime of another State. . . .[30]

Using these documents, Blum concludes that the Arab support of Palestinian terrorist groups is illegal under international law.

This conclusion of Blum and other international legal experts was sharply attacked during the United Nations debates on terrorism in the fall of 1972. A number of Third World legal authorities claimed that the activities of groups such as the Palestinians and the

African liberation movements were not terrorism but rather were struggles for national self-determination and hence were legal under international law. Consider the following passages from speeches in the Legal Committee of the General Assembly:

Cameroon

The delegation of Cameroon stood ready to co-operate in the search for measures to prevent terrorism and violence. "Terrorism," however, was not an accepted term of positive international law, and his delegation would have had misgivings as to its content had it not been for the Secretariat study. It could not accept a definition which would include as international terrorism the activities of liberation movements in colonial territories under foreign domination.[31]

Somalia

A clear distinction must be maintained between terrorism and the struggle of peoples for their freedom and independence, between terrorism and the determination to end injustices of historic proportions, and between terrorism and the struggle to obtain basic human rights.[32]

The international legal confusion over terrorism is compounded by a second controversy: What recourse does a state that is the victim of attack by terrorists have with regard to the state backing or tolerating the terrorists? Specifically, does a state that suffers from terrorist attacks have the right to undertake reprisals against the nation harboring the terrorist group?

The question of the legality of reprisals has been debated in the context of the Middle East by two international lawyers in the aftermath of the Israeli reprisal against the Beirut airport in December 1968. In an article entitled "The Beirut Raid and the International Law of Retaliation," Richard A. Falk argued that the Beirut reprisal was a violation of international law because it involved the use of force without any recourse to diplomatic solutions and because the Israelis failed to establish a direct link between the Lebanese government and the Palestinian terrorists.[33] Falk did not claim that all reprisals were forbidden by international law, but he laid down a series of strict preconditions that would have to be met before any reprisal could legally be undertaken:

A. That a diligent effort be made to achieve a pacific resolution over a reasonable period of time, including recourse to international organizations.
B. That the use of force is proportional to the provocation.
C. That the retaliatory action be directed against military and paramilitary targets.
D. That the government undertaking the reprisal provide an immediate explanation of its conduct before relevant international organs.[34]

Falk's requirements are sufficiently stringent so as to make most Israeli reprisals illegal.

Yehuda Z. Blum in a reply argued that Israeli attacks on Arab states supporting terrorism were legal because of the existing state of war between Israel and its Arab neighbors. Blum said that the Arabs were in effect waging war against Israel by backing terrorists organizations, and consequently under the legal right of self-defense Israel could retaliate against the Arab states.[35]

* * *

A fourth manner in which transnational terrorism has affected international relations is that the emergence of terrorist groups on the world scene provides an opportunity for a new form of international conflict, what Brian Jenkins of the RAND Corporation calls "surrogate warfare." By surrogate warfare Jenkins means the backing of terrorist groups by one nation or nations for the purpose of staging attacks against another nation or nations. Jenkins argues that certain conditions in the contemporary world make this option of surrogate warfare an attractive means of carrying on conflicts.[36]

One important attraction of surrogate warfare is simply that the alternatives have major drawbacks. Nuclear war, whether between the existing nuclear powers or between existing and future nuclear weapons states, would be extraordinarily destructive. For the foreseeable future any nation initiating nuclear attacks would run a major risk of inviting nuclear destruction either from the victims of the attack or, if the victim had no nuclear weapons, from any nuclear-armed allies of the victim state. Conventional war, while not as destructive as nuclear war, also has two major drawbacks: (a) it is an expensive proposition to put together a significant conventional capability, and (b) invasions with conventional forces have rather low legitimacy in the present world—in every major outbreak of conventional fighting in recent years there have been strong and usually successfully international efforts to get an immediate ceasefire.[37]

Surrogate warfare lacks these drawbacks to nuclear and conventional warfare and thus has a definite attractiveness. Since terrorism in the past has helped cause conflicts to escalate to major wars, a nation that resorted to surrogate warfare could set off a process of escalation that could reach the nuclear level. But the risks of all-out nuclear war are much less if one starts on the lower rungs of a ladder of escalation by resorting to low-level violence than if one starts at a high rung on the ladder of violence by using nuclear weapons.[38] The drawbacks involved with the "illegitimacy" of conventional warfare also are absent. The 1972 United Nations debates on terrorism show that to a large majority of the nations of the world terrorist campaigns, unlike conventional warfare, enjoy a high degree of legitimacy.[39] Finally, terrorist campaigns are nowhere near as expensive as conventional warfare.[40] In addition to lacking the drawbacks of nuclear and conventional warfare, surrogate warfare has special advantages of its own. For a limited investment a government can force an adversary to expend a large amount of resources in defense: Israeli countermeasures against the Palestinian guerrillas between the 1967 and 1973 wars cost Israel forty times what the 1967 war did.[41] And a government supporting a terrorist campaign against another state can always disclaim responsibility by maintaining that the terrorist organization it is supporting is completely independent of it. In any case, there have been numerous instances of surrogate warfare in recent years. Some examples follow.

For a period in 1968-1969 King Hussein of Jordan covertly backed al Fatah's attempts to conduct guerrilla and terrorist operations on the West Bank. Hussein and Arafat were both afraid that the Israelis were moving toward setting up a Palestinian state on the West Bank that would be under the control of neither of them. So Hussein, while continuing to denounce al Fatah in public, privately

supported Arafat's efforts to build an effective underground movement on the West Bank. Hussein and Arafat hoped that if sufficient
unrest and disorder could be created on the West Bank, the Israelis
would agree to relinquish their control.[42]

Between August 1969 and April 1970 members of the government of the Republic of Ireland gave covert aid in the form of
money, arms, and training to the Provisional IRA. This aid had
three basic purposes: (a) in the short run to protect the Ulster Catholic
community from attacks by Protestant mobs such as those which
took place in August 1969 and (b) to weaken the radical IRA (later
known as the Officials) and (c) in the long run to promote a united
Ireland.[43]

Prior to its massive conventional intervention in June 1976, Syria
sought to influence the course of events in the Lebanese civil war by
means of the al-Sa'iqa Palestinian group. Syria had founded and
had complete control of al-Sa'iqa. It used al-Sa'iqa to fight against
whichever faction it was seeking to defeat in the various stages of the
Lebanese civil war.[44]

Finally, governments are not the only parties who may find
resorting to surrogate warfare attractive. "Established" revolutionary movements such as the PLO that have many of the trap-
pings of statehood, such as offices in various nations and observer
status in international organizations, have felt it advisable to set up
small, allegedly independent groups to carry out actions of the sort
that the parent group could not carry out without damaging its
international reputation. This appears to have been the origin of
Black September, for there is substantial evidence that Black September was always under the control of Arafat and the PLO and
that the whole purpose of setting up Black September was to stage
spectacular acts of terrorism against Israel, such as the Munich
Olympics incident, without having to suffer international condemnation.[45]

It is also important to note that this new form of conflict affects
nations unequally. Totalitarian societies such as China and the
Soviet Union are much less vulnerable to disruption by terrorists
than are democratic systems, not because such societies are more
just or because they have less social conflict, but because they are
much more capable of coercing and controlling their populations.[46]

In other words, surrogate warfare is a new weapon in the arsenals of nondemocratic powers—a new weapon that if skillfully exploited can give them a definite advantage. The August 1975 "Carlos" affair in Paris illustrates the use by totalitarian states of surrogate warfare. An informer led three French police agents to an apartment in Paris where Ilich Ramirez Sanchez, alias "Carlos," was hiding. When the police attempted to arrest him, Carlos pulled out a submachine gun, killed the informer and two of the policemen, seriously wounded the third, and then fled. He left behind him documents indicating that he was being used by Cuban intelligence to coordinate shipments of arms and money to various terrorist movements around the world, including the Baader-Meinhof group, the Japanese United Red Army, and the PFLP.[47]

* * *

A fifth impact of terrorism on international relations can be seen as yet only in embryonic form, if it in fact is a real possibility at all: the prospect that terrorism may lead to the destruction of international order. Concern is frequently expressed that the ability of terrorists to disrupt society is going up steadily as the technology of modern weaponry becomes more and more diffused. In the area of conventional armaments such technological innovations as hand-held, antiaircraft missiles and miniature submachine guns open up new possibilities for terrorists to cause destruction.[48] And with the steady proliferation of peaceful nuclear energy, there is an increasing danger of terrorists getting access to nuclear weapons.[49] The result of this increased disruptive capability could be that governments will no longer be able to provide adequate protection for their citizens. In consequence people may well take action themselves. Terrorism will be met with counter-terrorism. There would be a return to private wars on the medieval model with terrorists and counter-terrorists battling it out all over the globe.[50]

These tendencies toward international anarchy are only incipient now, where they exist at all. There have been instances of wars between terrorists and counter-terrorists: the terrorism of the Palestinian groups has produced a response in the form of attacks on Arab and Russian targets by the Jewish Defense League (JDL). The actions of the Basque independence movement (the ETA) have led to counter-terrorism against Basques living in France by members of a Spanish extreme rightist group called the Guerrillas of Christ the King.[51] In the Algerian war FLN terrorism led to the counter-terrorism of the OAS. In Ulster the Provisional IRA and the Protestant paramilitary groups are engaged in a seemingly endless series of attacks and reprisals against each other. And the technological dangers, while often exaggerated in sensationalist popular literature, are very real.

There are, however, countervailing factors that may arrest any drift toward such a breakdown. First, there is the fact that among the world's revolutionary movements the willingness to cause enormous destruction using sophisticated technology and the ability to get hold of such technology seem to be inversely related. The large, well-organized, and well-financed national liberation groups engaged in guerrilla and terrorist campaigns, such as the Palestine Liberation Organization, the Provisional Irish Republican Army, and the Zimbabwe nationalists are basically interested in liberating some particular small corner of the world; rhetoric aside, they have no interest in world revolution.[52] Second, these organizations rely upon support from members of the international community in their efforts to attain their goals. The PLO is financed and armed by the Arab states and the Soviet Union, the Provisional IRA has a network of sympathizers in the United States who supply money and guns, and the Zimbabwe nationalists are dependent for bases of operation on the African countries that border Rhodesia. If any of these groups were to get hold of and use highly destructive weapons, they would run the risk of being branded as international outlaws.

And third, such revolutionary movements have popular constituencies that could be subjected to retaliation if they were to engage in indiscriminate killing of their opponents' nationals. The PLO is based on Palestinians living both inside and outside of Israeli-controlled territory, the IRA seeks support from Catholics in Ulster and in the Republic of Ireland, and the Zimbabwe nationalists claim to represent the black population of Rhodesia. Because local revolutionary movements have no interest in worldwide upheaval, need some degree of international legitimacy and recognition, and have constituencies that could be attacked, the larger organizations are not likely to want to get hold of weapons of mass destruction, whether chemical, biological, or nuclear, although they might well be able to do so if they wanted to.

There are terrorist organizations which, unlike the groups mentioned above, *do* seek massive destruction and upheaval to attain their goals. George Habash, the leader of the PFLP, was asked, "Does it matter to you that the Middle East crisis might develop into a World War?" He replied: "Not really. The word has forgotten Palestine. Now it must pay attention to our struggles."[53] At his trial Kozo Okamoto, the only survivor of the three-man terrorist squad that carried out the killings at Lod Airport in May 1972, stated:

The revolutionary struggle is a political struggle between the classes. It is a just struggle. We strive to build a world in which wars will be banished. But it will be a long struggle and we are preparing World War III through killing people, destroying houses, annihilating property. . . .

War involves slaughtering and destruction. We cannot limit warfare to the destruction of buildings. We believe slaughtering of human bodies is inevitable. We know that it will become even more severe than battles between nations.[54]

While groups such as the PFLP and the United Red Army are extreme in their methods and their goals, they also are small as compared to groups like the PLO, the Provisional IRA, and the Zimbabwe nationalists. The PFLP is considerably smaller than al Fatah or al-Sa'iqa, the two major members of the PLO.[55] The United Red Army may number as few as three dozen members.[56] Thus, although these groups may well be willing to cause massive destruction with sophisticated technology, their ability to acquire such technology is restricted by their small size.

A second factor that should be considered in any evaluation of the chances for a breakdown of international order is that, if such a breakdown appears imminent, the community of nations may well abandon its differences over the question of terrorism and unite to meet the threat to international order. One of the reasons why terrorism has flourished is that the international response to the problem has been feeble at best. Many nations are indifferent, and several provide active support for various transnational terrorist organizations. Yet there is reason to doubt that this tolerant attitude would continue if terrorism became a genuine danger to the present world order.

For example, for years there was only a slow and uncertain response to the problem of hijackings, but when they became so numerous as to threaten civil aviation there was a determined international reaction. Three multilateral anti-hijacking accords were negotiated: one in Tokyo (1963), one in The Hague (1970), and one in Montreal (1971). (All three have received enough ratifications to come into effect.) Airport and airline security and screening procedures were considerably tightened up. Two nations without diplomatic relations and generally on very poor terms, the United States and Cuba, were able to set aside their mutual hostility and sign a bilateral accord on hijacking in February 1973. The result of this international response was that the phenomenon of hijackings, which seemed in 1969-1970 to pose a mortal threat to civil aviation, had by 1975 largely been brought under control: there were eight successful hijackings in 1974, compared to seventy in 1969 and forty-six in 1970.[57] Thus, when it has perceived its interests seriously enough threatened, the international community has reacted forcefully to certain manifestations of terrorism.

NOTES

1. Carol Baumann, *The Diplomatic Kidnappings* (The Hague: Martinus Nijhoff, 1973), pp. 99-100.

2. Brian M. Jenkins and Janera Johnson, *International Terrorism: A Chronology, 1968-1974* (Santa Monica, California: The RAND Corporation, R-1597-DOS/ARPA, 1975), p. 23; Baumann, *Diplomatic Kidnappings*, p. 162. Dias Gomide was kidnapped on the same day that Daniel Mitrione was abducted.

3. *Jerusalem Post*, October 7 and 13, 1975. Claustre was finally released in February 1977.

4. *London Times*, May 27, 1975; *Boston Globe*, June 29, 1975; and *New York Times*, June 26, 1975.

5. Jenkins and Johnson, *Terrorism Chronology*, p. 35.

6. *New York Times*, October 30, 1972.

7. *New York Times*, October 31, 1972.

8. Walter Z. Laqueur, *Confrontation: The Middle East and World Politics* (New York: Bantam Books, 1974), p. 58; see also Christopher Dobson, *Black September* (New York: The Macmillan Company, 1974), pp. 10-11.

9. *Washington Post*, August 31, 1974.

10. *Washington Post*, September 26, 1974.

11. Dobson, *Black September*, p. 86.

12. Sidney B. Fay, *The Origins of the World War* (New York: The Free Press, 1966), pp. 86-87.

13. Ibid., p. 145.

14. Ibid., pp. 550-551.

15. A. J. P. Taylor, *The Struggle for Mastery in Europe, 1848-1918* (Oxford: The Clarendon Press, 1954), pp. 523.

16. See Taylor, *Struggle*, pp. 450-452, 455, and 490-500, for a discussion of the antagonism between Serbia and Austria-Hungary in the context of general European diplomacy in the years leading up to World War I.

17. Fay, *Origins*, p. 558.

18. Interview No. 42 (Ze'ev Schiff).

19. Yair Evron, *The Middle East: Nations, Superpowers, and Wars* (New York: Praeger Publishers, 1973), pp. 72-73; and Interview No. 42 (Ze'ev Schiff). The Samu raid came as part of a series of reprisals sparked by the beginning of al Fatah's military activities against Israel in early 1965.

20. Interview No. 37 (Dan Horowitz).

21. Evron, *The Middle East*, p. 38.

22. Moshe Dayan, *Diary of the Sinai Campaign* (New York: Harper & Row, 1966), p. 5.

23. Evron, *The Middle East*, p. 74.

24. Walter Z. Laqueur, *The Road to Jerusalem* (New York: The Macmillan Company, 1968), pp. 81-82.

25. Interview No. 42 (Ze'ev Schiff).

26. Laqueur, *Jerusalem*, p. 232 and passim.

27. For an exhaustive documentation of the hostility, see Y. Harkabi, *Arab Attitudes to Israel* (New York: Hart Publishing Company, Inc., 1972).

28. See Yehuda Z. Blum, "The Beirut Raid and the International Double Standard: A Reply to Professor Richard A. Falk," *The Arab-Israeli Conflict*, Vol. II, ed. John Norton Moore (Princeton, New Jersey: Princeton University Press, 1974), passim.

29. Ibid., p. 257.

30. Ibid., p. 258.

31. *Official Records of the General Assembly*, 6th Committee, 27th

Session, 1359 Meeting, p. 273.

32. Ibid., 1363 Meeting, p. 293.

33. Richard A. Falk, "The Beirut Raid and the International Law of Retaliation," in *Great Issues of International Politics,* ed. Morton A. Kaplan (Chicago: Aldine Publishing Company, 1970), p. 57.

34. Ibid. See pp. 58-59 for a detailed breakdown of Falk's preconditions for legally initiating a reprisal.

35. Blum, "Double Standard," pp. 254-255.

36. Brian Jenkins, *International Terrorism: A New Mode of Conflict* (Los Angeles, California: Crescent Publications, 1975), pp. 19-22.

37. Ibid., p. 20. This was the case in the 1967 and 1973 Middle Eastern wars, in the 1971 India-Pakistan war, and in the Turkish invasion of Cyprus in 1974.

38. On Herman Kahn's "escalation ladder" of some 44 steps, with Step 44 being all-out nuclear warfare against cities, Step 8 being the use of terrorism, and Step 21 being the "nuclear threshold," that is, the use of nuclear weapons. See Herman Kahn, *On Escalation* (Baltimore, Maryland: Penguin Books, 1965), pp. 73 and 94-133.

39. *Official Records of the General Assembly,* 6th Committee, 27th Session, passim.

40. Jenkins, *International Terrorism,* p. 21.

41. Ibid., p. 21.

42. Ehud Yaari, *Strike Terror* (New York: Sabra Books, 1970), pp. 241-242. Hussein abandoned his support of the *fedayeen* in mid-1969 when he began to perceive them as a threat to the stability of his own regime.

43. J. Bower Bell, *The Secret Army: The IRA, 1916-1974* (Cambridge, Massachusetts: The M.I.T. Press, 1974), pp. 370-371. This support of the Provisionals came to an end in May 1970 after its existence was revealed.

44. Interview No. 4 (Rehoboam Ze'ev). The Lebanese civil war broke out in the spring of 1975. The fighting was terminated at least for the present by the establishment of an Arab peace-keeping force in the fall of 1976.

45. Interview No. 4 (Rehoboam Ze'ev); Dobson, *Black September,* passim; and Rolf Tophaven, *Fedayin* (Munich: Bernard and Graefe Verlag fur Wehrwessen, 1974), p. 93.

46. For an incisive discussion of this issue see Walter Z. Laqueur, "Diversities of Violence and the Current World System," in *Civil Violence and International Politics* (London: The International Institute for Strategic Studies, 1971), pp. 14-16.

47. *New York Times,* August 17, 1975; and *Boston Globe,* August 5, 1975.

48. Brian Jenkins, "High Technology Terrorism and Surrogate Warfare:

The Impact of New Technology on Low-Level Violence" (Santa Monica, California: The RAND Corporation, 1975), passim.

49. Theodore Taylor and Mason Willrich, *Nuclear Theft: Risks and Safeguards* (Cambridge, Massachusetts: Ballinger Publishing Company, 1974), passim.

50. Brian Jenkins, *International Terrorism*, p. 24; Hedley Bull, "Civil Violence and International Order," *Civil Violence and the International System* (London: International Institute for Strategic Studies, 1971), p. 31.

51. *London Times*, June 7, 1975.

52. J. Bowyer Bell, "Contemporary Revolutionary Organizations," in *Transnational Relations and World Order*, ed. Robert O. Keohane and Joseph S. Nye (Cambridge, Massachusetts: Harvard University Press, 1972), p. 167.

53. Dobson, *Black September*, p. 62.

54. Ibid., p. 74.

55. *The Washington Post*, December 2, 1974.

56. Fay Willey, "New-Look Rogue's Gallery," *Newsweek*, January 5, 1975, p. 28.

57. *Strategy Survey, 1974* (London: International Institute for Strategic Studies, 1975), p. 90.

PART II: American Policy Response to International Terrorism

The best hope of justice
lies in the fact that a stable
order is not possible without
introducing instruments of justice
into the agreements which are to
provide for order.

*The Children of Light and the
Children of Darkness*
by Reinhold Niebuhr

chapter 5
DETERRENCE LITERATURE AND TERRORISM

Alexander George and Richard Smoke suggest that deterrence is the art of convincing an opponent that the costs and risks of a particular course of action outweigh the benefits: that C (costs) $+$ R (risks) $>B$ (benefits).[1] Deterrence can be achieved in one or both of two ways: one can raise the $C + R$ side of the formula by threatening deleterious consequences for a particular course of action (deterrence by punishment), or one can lower the B side of the formula by denying the adversary any gains from his actions (deterrence by denial).[2] American national security policy has made use of deterrence by both punishment and denial. The mission of the American strategic nuclear forces is to achieve deterrence by punishment of any Soviet or Chinese nuclear attack on the United States by being able to destroy an unacceptably high portion of the Soviet or Chinese population and industry in retaliation for such an attack. The American forces in South Korea are an example of deterrence by denial: the rationale for the presence of these forces is that they deter North Korean aggression by convincing them that the United States will use military force to prevent North Korea from invading South Korea.

Deterrence is a very old concept, although it was not until recent times that this concept was clearly understood and elaborated upon. Thomas Schelling in *Arms and Influence* used historical examples of rulers achieving their aims by threatening punishment:

A. At one point in the course of the struggle between the Greeks and the Persians in the fifth century B.C. the Persians sent ambassadors to some Ionian cities with the following instructions:

. . . make your proposals to them and promise that, if they will abandon their allies, there will be no disagreeable consequences for them; we will not set fire to their houses or temples, or threaten them with any greater harshness than before this trouble occurred. If, however, they refuse, and insist upon fighting, then you must resort to threats, and say exactly what we will do to them; tell them, that is, that when they are beaten they will be sold as slaves, their boys will be made eunuchs, their girls carried off to Bactria, and their land confiscated.[3]

B. Jenghis Khan, in the course of his far-flung campaigns on the Eurasian land mass, frequently used the stratagem of forcing captives—including women, children, and old people—to march ahead of his army and thus be made the first casualties in the event of any resistance by the fellow citizens of the captives.[4]

C. The strategy of threatening punishment to attain one's aims was forcefully and eloquently expressed by Shakespeare in the following speech by Henry V before the gates of Harfleur:

> We may as bootless spend our vain command
> Upon the enraged soldiers in their spoil
> As send precepts to the leviathan
> To come ashore. Therefore, you men of Harfleur,
> Take pity of your town and of your people,
> Whiles yet my soldiers are in my command
> Whiles yet the cool and temperate wind of grace
> O'erblows the filthy and contagious clouds
> Of heady murder, spoil and villainry.
> If not, why, in a moment look to see
> The blind and bloody soldier with foul hand
> Defile the locks of your shrill-shrieking daughters;
> Your fathers taken by the silver beard,
> And their most reverent heads dash'd to the walls,
> Your naked infants spitted upon pikes,
> Whiles the mad mothers with their howls confused
> Do break the clouds . . .
> What say you? will you yield, and this avoid,
> Or, guilty in defence, be thus destroy'd?[5]

However, while the use of violence to hurt and destroy to attain one's ends is an old concept, a clear distinction between deterrence, getting one's aims by convincing an adversary to give in, and force, seizing what you want by physical power, was not developed until the twentieth century. George and Smoke maintain that what deterrence as a concept had always lacked up to the interwar years and did not clearly have until the development of nuclear weapons was a sharp radical distinction between the power to hurt and the power to defeat military forces. They argue that for Thucydides, Machiavelli, and the "limited warriors" of the eighteenth and nineteenth centuries, it was generally impossible to seriously hurt an enemy until after one had defeated its military forces.[6]

Historical examples of deterrence bear out this argument. For the Persians to be able to devastate the Ionian cities they first had to be able to capture them. When he initially invaded a country Jenghis Khan presumably did not have any of the citizens of that country as captives. He could get captives only after the invasion had progressed, which meant that he first would have to defeat at least some of his opponents' military forces. And for Henry V to execute his terrible threats against Harfleur he first had to besiege the city.

The concept of deterrence has been widely analyzed and discussed since 1945. Herman Kahn argues that in foreign policy there are three types of deterrence. Type I is deterrence of a direct attack on one's country, for example, the American threat to destroy Soviet cities in the event of a nuclear attack on American cities. Type II is the use of strategic threats to deter what Kahn calls "acts of extreme provocation," that is, acts that are deemed threatening to the country in question but do not involve direct attacks on the country itself. An example is the American pledge to resort to nuclear attacks on the Soviet Union if such attacks are necessary to prevent Western Europe from being conquered by the Soviet Union. Type III is what Kahn calls "tit-for-tat" or graduated, controlled deterrence. Here the opponent is deterred by the threat that the defender will take limited actions, both military and nonmilitary, to make the aggression unprofitable. Examples are some of the American efforts in Vietnam, ranging from the bombing of North Vietnam at one extreme to pacification programs at the other (the extremes being defined by the intensity of the violence involved).[7]

George and Smoke also argue that there are three levels of deterrence in American foreign policy (their three levels bear a definite resemblance to Herman Kahn's three types). The first is the deterrent relationship between the strategic nuclear arsenals of the two superpowers. The second is the deterrence of limited conventional war and aggression against the allies of the United States. The third is deterrence of what are called "sublimited" conflicts, that is, conflicts at the low end of the scale of violence.[8] They argue that the literature on deterrence has been heavily skewed in the direction of the first level of deterrence, with only a fairly small amount of work being done concerning the second level (mostly centering around the contingency of a Soviet conventional attack in Central Europe) and with almost no theoretical work on the third level.

They explain this skewing by first noting that the first level is an issue of more pressing concern to the United States than the second and similarly the second level is more pressing than the third. Given the enormous destructive potential of the Soviet nuclear arsenal, it was imperative for American policy makers to come up with a means of preventing nuclear war between the superpowers. If such a war could not be prevented, then none of the other goals and aims of American foreign policy were very relevant. While not as pressing as the need to prevent an American-Soviet nuclear war, the deterrence of a Soviet invasion of Western Europe ranked high on the list of American foreign policy priorities. Deterrence of conventional aggression in other regions of the world did not have the immediacy of the need to prevent a war in Central Europe. The threats to American national interest being posed by "sublimited" conflicts or surrogate warfare were not pressing enough to have received the degree of scholarly attention devoted to the others.[9]

Second, they suggest that the higher the level of deterrence, the easier the problem is from an analytical point of view.[10] Deterrence theory becomes much more complex as one goes down the levels. More and more variables are added. And the variables become harder and harder to measure. (See Table III, reproduced from George and Smoke's book.)

A third reason why the deterrence of sublimited, low-level violence has not been studied much may be that prevailing academic ideological currents arising from the impact of the war in Vietnam have discouraged such research. In the emotion-charged Vietnam years any sort of policy-relevant studies on low-level violence ran the risk of being branded by student radicals and antiwar academics as "counter-insurgency" studies and hence a blot on the good name of the university. The result has been that serious, empirical, policy-relevant work on low-level violence became uncommon in American universities after the mid-1960s.

It has only been since about 1975 that there has been a revival of empirical and policy-oriented work on the topic of political violence. There are two factors that have led to this revival: the termination of direct American involvement in Indochina has ended the emotionally charged campus atmosphere, and the appearance of international terrorism on a significant scale has forced a number of scholars to take heed of such political violence. So for the first time since the wave of counter-insurgency studies in the early 1960s, there is serious work being done on low-level conflicts.

There are, of course, several problems in applying deterrence literature to the problem of international terrorism. A first objection might run as follows: this body of literature was developed for the purpose of analyzing state-to-state conflicts and cannot be applied without major modifications to conflicts between states and revolutionary movements. Yet as long as a conflict exists between two rational opponents, deterrence literature can be applied. After all, while the basic focus of deterrence literature has been toward state-to-state conflicts at the upper levels of deterrence (especially the deterrence relationship between the superpowers), many of the examples that deterrence theorists such as Kahn and Schelling draw on are from situations that do not involve states. Schelling notes at several points in *Arms and Influence* that the strategy of the cavalry against the Indians during the plains wars was not to totally defeat the Indians in a military sense, because such a course of action, while within the capability of the cavalry, would have been excessively costly in manpower and money. Instead, the cavalry followed a strategy of punitive raids against Indian camps and villages in instances where the Indians went off the reservation to raid settlements.[11] Schelling also points out that in the 1920s and 1930s the British kept Arabian tribes in their various Middle Eastern possessions under control by carrying out air strikes against the villages

TABLE III.   *A Checklist of Varying Characteristics of Deterrence*

	LEVEL ONE	LEVEL TWO	LEVEL THREE
Own objectives			
Number	One	Few	Many
Are they in conflict with each other?	—	Sometimes	Usually
Are such conflicts serious and difficult to resolve?	—	Sometimes	Often
How motivated should one be?	Totally	Uncertain	Very Uncertain
Opponent's objectives			
Number	One	Few	Many
Are they clear?	Yes	Often	Rarely
Is it clear what their limits are?	Yes	Rarely	Hardly ever
Is it clear how motivated he is to attain them?	Yes	Rarely	Hardly ever
Own Means			
Number of kinds appropriate	Basically one	Very few	Many
Criteria for selection among	—	Fairly clear	Unclear
Criteria for selection of quantity	Clear	Fairly clear	Unclear
Opponent's Means			
Number of kinds	Basically one	Very few	Many
Difficulty in estimating which means or how much he will use	None	Often some	Usually considerable
Degree of polarization of actual or potential conflict	Absolute	Acute	Variable and mixed
General ambiguity in the situation	Very little	Sometimes considerable	Usually very great

TABLE III. (Cont.)

	LEVEL ONE	LEVEL TWO	LEVEL THREE
Number of other national policies that intersect with the deterrence policy	Very few	A number	Many
Likelihood of conflicts among these policies that will be difficult to resolve	No	Sometimes	Usually
How many possible outcomes are there to the situation	Very few	Moderately few	A great many
Does a crisis in deterrence last long enough to alter many of the above-mentioned variables and considerations?	No	Yes	Yes
Is the nature of "rationality" in dealing with the crisis problematical?	No	Slightly	Considerably
Uncertainties	Minimal	Considerable	Enormous

Source: Reprinted from A. L. George and R. Smoke, *Deterrence in American Foreign Policy: Theory and Practice*, New York: Columbia University Press, 1974, pp. 52-53, by permission of the publisher.

of any rebellious tribes.[12] In other words, both the American cavalry and the Royal Air Force were following a strategy of deterrence through punishment.

Herman Kahn has made use of the sport of "chicken" as an analogy to illustrate certain facts about nuclear confrontations between the superpowers. Specifically, he notes that just as in "chicken" the best way to win is to make oneself seem totally irrational (and hence unwilling to swerve out of the way of the oncoming car) by taking the steering wheel out of the car or by being drunk while driving, so too in international affairs there is the logic of the "rationality of the irrational." By seeming to be irrational one can gain an edge over an opponent: he will feel that there is no chance the other party will act reasonably, so the burden of avoiding a disaster is his alone.[13]

Second, do terrorist groups have a sufficient degree of rationality in their behavior for deterrence theory, which assumes rational behavior, to be applied? George and Smoke argue that rationality is a collection of five attributes. First, the value hierarchy of the actor, whether a nation, a group, or an individual, has to be internally consistent. Second, the actor must be able to assess the outcomes of his actions; even if his values are internally consistent, he will not be able to attain them unless he can evaluate outcomes and decide which of them are consistent with his values. Third, the actor must decide what actions on his part are likely to generate any particular outcome. In other words, even if the actor's values are internally consistent and even if he knows which outcomes are desirable in light of those values, there is still the problem of choosing the course of action that will lead to the preferred outcome. Fourth, there is the problem of information: very often an actor lacks the information necessary to evaluate outcomes or to assess the course of action required to achieve the desired outcome. Fifth, there is the problem of estimating an opponent's payoffs: in the real world, unlike in game theory, the opponent does not provide one with a matrix of his payoffs. An actor has to estimate what a fairly consistent value hierarchy for the opponent might be, how he connects this value hierarchy to his various perceived outcomes, what actions he may decide can serve a given outcome, and what information he has available to him—in all these respects the actor's knowledge about his opponent may be seriously deficient. They go on to argue that given the difficulty of meeting these conditions, rationality is a condition to be striven for and approximated rather than assumed to exist.[14]

Terrorist groups would appear to meet these conditions of rationality to a sufficient degree for deterrence theory to be applied. First, a frequent misapprehension about terrorist groups is that their violence is mindless and purposeless. However, such violence in the main is quite purposive: it seeks to attain a valued objective, whether the liberation of one's homeland (as in the case of the IRA, EOKA, and Irgun), or the smashing of international imperialism (as in the case of the PFLP and the United Red Army).

Second, there are five goals for terroristic acts: publicity, harassment of the authorities, polarization of society, aggravation of state-to-state relations, and the securing of prisoners and ransoms. The fact that the leaders and theoreticians of terrorist groups have spelled out these goals in documents, memoirs, and interviews demonstrates that they are able to evaluate outcomes and decide which ones will lead to the attainment of their values. For example, the remarks cited earlier by Leila Khaled of the PFLP and General George Grivas of EOKA indicate that they had considered the question of publicity and decided it was essential to the success of their cause.[15]

As for the third attribute of rationality—that the actor in question knows which actions will lead to an outcome consistent with his values—the large number of terrorist movements in recent years and the vast number of incidents that these groups have staged has led to the creation of a "data bank" which can be used to judge the effects of terrorist actions. That terrorists do assess different courses of action and adopt the seemingly productive ones can be documented by looking at the history of diplomatic kidnappings. There was only one attempted diplomatic kidnapping in 1968. Then in 1969 the widely publicized kidnapping of Charles Burke Elbrick, the American ambassador to Brazil, took place. The utility of the tactic of diplomatic kidnappings had been demonstrated, and the result was widespread imitation: in 1970 there was a total of eighteen attempts to kidnap diplomats.[16]

Fourth, concerning the information available to terrorists about the effectiveness of their actions—given that terrorist incidents usually spark a round of stories in the communications media about the reactions to the incident of the government, of the public, and of the international community—the terrorists do have available to them enough information to be able to meet the other four attributes of rationality.

Finally, as for the problem of being able to evaluate the payoff matrix of an opponent, the evidence is that in a number of instances terrorist groups have successfully estimated an opponent's payoffs. For example, two years before the beginning of the Cyprus insurgency General Grivas wrote a memorandum in which he argued that the unfavorable international publicity for Great Britain his campaign would generate would terminate British colonial control of Cyprus. The unfavorable publicity the campaign produced clearly was one of the factors that led Britain to grant Cyprus its independence.[17] The kidnapping by the ETA of the West German consul in San Sebastian in 1970 was also an instance of a group correctly calculating an opponent's payoff matrix: Generalissimo Francisco Franco commuted the death sentences of six Basque terrorists in return for the release of the consul.[18] Of course, like nations and individuals, terrorists can misjudge an opponent at times. Witness the disastrous consequences for the Uruguayan Tupamaros of their strategy of provoking governmental repression: the government became so repressive that it was able to destroy the Tupamaros. And the terrorists who hijacked an Air France airliner to Entebbe airport in Uganda fatally miscalculated the Israeli willingness and ability to use force to free the hostages.

Another problem in the application of deterrence theory to the issue of international terrorism is that terrorist groups differ radically from each other, and so it is difficult to have a single deterrence policy that will deter very many of them. There has been an unfortunate tendency among the media to lump all terrorist groups together when in reality many of the groups have little in common. In particular, there has been a marked failure by the press to make a distinction between groups with universal, global goals, such as the United Red Army and PFLP, and groups with limited, nationalistic goals, such as the IRA and al Fatah.

While these differences among terrorist groups are very real, at the same time there are important similarities among a large number of them. There are, for example, a common set of ideological heroes: Fanon, Guevara, and Marighella.[19] Another similarity among terrorist groups is that they adopt successful tactics from one another. These similarities do not mean that it is possible to develop a policy that will effectively deter all groups. What these similarities do indicate is that a large number of terrorist groups have enough in common so that a policy developed in response to one group's actions, if successful against that group, also quite possibly will work with other groups. The empirical problem is how to develop a set of policies that will deter a significant number of terrorist groups.

NOTES

1. Alexander George and Richard Smoke, *Deterrence in American Foreign Policy: Theory and Practice* (New York: Columbia University Press, 1974), p. 48.

2. Ibid., p. 134.

3. Herodotus, *The Histories*, trans. Aubrey de Selincourt (Baltimore, Maryland: Penguin Books, 1954), p. 362; quoted in Thomas Schelling, *Arms and Influence* (New Haven, Connecticut: Yale University Press, 1966), pp. 10-11.

4. Schelling, *Arms and Influence*, p. 6.

5. *Henry V*, Act III, Scene iii, quoted in Schelling, *Arms and Influence*, p. 11.

6. George and Smoke, *Deterrence*, p. 21.

7. Herman Kahn, *On Thermonuclear War* (New York: The Free Press, 1969), p. 126.

8. George and Smoke, *Deterrence*, pp. 38-39.

9. Ibid., p. 47.

10. Ibid., p. 49.

11. Schelling, *Arms and Influence*, pp. 5, 14-15.

12. Ibid., pp. 13-14.

13. Kahn, *On Thermonuclear War*, pp. 291-295.

14. George and Smoke, *Deterrence*, pp. 74-75.

15. George Grivas, *The Memoirs of General Grivas* (New York: Frederick A. Praeger, 1965), p. 204; Leila Khaled, *My People Shall Live* (London: Hodden and Staughton, 1973), p. 214.

16. Brian M. Jenkins and Janera Johnson, *International Terrorism: A Chronology, 1968-1974* (Santa Monica, California: The RAND Corporation, R-1597-DOS/ARPA, 1975), pp. 12-27.

17. Grivas, *Memoirs*, p. 204.

18. Jenkins and Johnson, *Terrorism Chronology*, p. 26.

19. Interviews No. 9 (Sir Geoffrey Jackson) and No. 33 (Sean Holly); Carlos Marighella, "The Minimanual of the Urban Guerrilla," appendix in Robert Moss, *Urban Guerrilla Warfare* (London: International Institute for Strategic Studies, 1971), p. 20.

chapter 6
DETERRENCE OF
HOSTAGE SITUATIONS

Given the current American policy toward hostage situations of "no concessions," it is easy to forget that when political kidnappings first became a frequent international phenomenon the American attitude toward such incidents was much more accommodating. For example, when Charles Burke Elbrick, the American ambassador to Brazil, was kidnapped in September 1969 the State Department put pressure on the Brazilian government to release the fifteen prisoners demanded as the condition for the ambassador's safe return.[1] When the Brazilians acceded to the terrorists' demands and the ambassador was returned unharmed, Secretary of State William Rogers issued a statement in which he expressed the gratitude of the United States to the Brazilians for having placed the safety of Elbrick "above all other considerations."[2] Similarly, when Sean Holly, U.S. labor attaché in Guatemala, was kidnapped in March 1970, the American government put pressure on the Guatemalan authorities to give in to the terrorists' demands. The Guatemalans acceded and freed the two prisoners whom the terrorists had asked for. Holly was released unharmed.[3]

In the latter half of 1970, however, American policy toward political kidnappings became less accommodating. When Agency for International Development adviser Daniel Mitrione was kidnapped by the Tupamaro guerrillas on July 31, 1970, the American government may have privately put some pressure on the Uruguayan authorities to meet part of the terrorists' demands,[4] but in public the United States supported the Uruguayans' refusal to release the 150 prisoners demanded by the Tupamaros.[5] Mitrione's body was found by the Uruguayan police on August 10, 1970.[6]

The intransigence indicated by the American government during the Mitrione incident was dramatically reaffirmed a month later when a TWA jetliner with a number of Americans on board was hijacked by the PFLP to Dawson field in Jordan. A Swissair jet and then a BOAC jet were also hijacked by the PFLP and diverted to Dawson field; both airliners contained a number of American passengers. The PFLP demanded the release of captured terrorists held by the British, German, Israeli, and Swiss governments. The PFLP did not ask the United States to release anyone, but it was clear that the hijackers wanted American hostages in the hope that the American government would put pressure on the other governments that were holding terrorists as prisoners.[7] The response by the American government to this multiple hijacking was to get all of the nations whose nationals were being held to issue a joint statement demanding the immediate and unconditional release of the hostages and the aircraft. Initially, all of the relevant nations did agree to demand such an unconditional release. But when the hijacking incident touched off the Jordanian civil war of 1970 the West European governments, fearful of the danger to their nationals from the fighting, became more willing to make concessions. Ultimately a deal was worked out whereby the British, Swiss, and West German governments released several captured *fedayeen*, and in return the hostages were released, although the planes were blown up.[8]

The "no concessions" policy of the United States that was demonstrated in the Mitrione case and in the September 1970 hijackings was reaffirmed several times in the course of the next few years. In early 1971 the Nixon administration's report on foreign policy for the next decade (entitled *U.S. Foreign Policy for the 1970's: Building for Peace*) reiterated the idea of a "no concessions" approach to hostage situations with the following remarks about aircraft hijacking: ". . . we need to make certain that there is no profit in such a crime, and no sanctuary for those who commit it."[9] And at the time of the Munich Olympics incident, the American government, through the medium of instructions issued by the Cabinet

Committee to Combat Terrorism, again indicated that the proper policy toward hostage situations was to refuse all concessions.[10]

Perhaps the most dramatic statement of American policy toward diplomatic kidnappings was produced by the Khartoum incident of March 1973. In this incident a number of diplomats attending a party at the Saudi Arabian embassy in Khartoum, including the American Ambassador Cleo Noel and his deputy Curtis Moore, were seized by a Black September squad. The terrorists demanded the release of Sirhan Sirhan (the assassin of Senator Robert Kennedy), of a large number of Palestinian guerrillas being held in Jordan, and of several members of the Baader-Meinhof group being held by the West Germans. When their demands were refused, the terrorists killed the two American diplomats and Belgian chargé d'affaires Guy Eid.[11] In the immediate aftermath of the incident the following widely publicized statements were made by Deputy Under Secretary of State William Macomber, who helped to handle several of the terrorist incidents of the 1970s, and by President Nixon:

Macomber:

You have to make it not only painful and risky personally for these people to mess around with Americans, but then you have got—and this is just terrible and coldblooded—but then you got to make it clear that there isn't going to be any reward. We are not going to pay blackmail. The president has made it clear, and he is dead right. Only when the world comes to this position is this terrible thing going to end.[12]

Nixon:

All of us would have liked to have saved the lives of these two very brave men, but they knew and we knew that in the event we paid international blackmail in this way, it would have saved their lives but it would have endangered the lives of hundreds of others all over the world, because once the individual, the terrorist, or the others has [sic] a demand that is made, that is satisfied, he then is encouraged to try it again, and that is why the position of your government has to be one in the interest of preserving life, of not submitting to international blackmail or extortion anyplace in the world.[13]

In the spring of 1974 the U.S. House of Representatives Internal Security Committee held a series of hearings on terrorism. In the course of these hearings Lewis Hoffacker, the special assistant to the Secretary of State for combatting terrorism, stated that while tactics varied in different hostage situations, in no instance would the U.S. government agree to pay ransom to kidnappers, nor would it agree to release prisoners. Hoffacker went on to say that the American government advised other governments, individuals, and companies to adopt a similar "no concessions" policy, because to do otherwise would be to increase terrorist incidents. Hoffacker claimed that a policy of firmness could save human lives not only in the long run but in the short run as well.[14]

In the spring and summer of 1975 there was a hostage situation that led to a significant public debate on American policy toward political kidnappings. The incident in question was the kidnapping of one Dutch and three American students in Tanzania in May by a Zaire-based terrorist group. The students were taken into Zaire and held for ransom. The parents of the students raised the ransom, and the students were released. It was soon revealed that Beverly Carter, the American ambassador to Tanzania, had helped in making the arrangements for the ransom to be paid, in defiance of the State Department's policy of "no concessions." Carter was reprimanded and denied an expected appointment as ambassador to Denmark.[15]

At two press conferences shortly after the reprimand of Ambassador Carter, Secretary of State Kissinger was asked about American policy toward political kidnappings. He replied that if terrorist groups get the impression that they can force an acquiescence in their demands, then lives may be saved at one place at the risk of hundreds of lives everywhere else. He stated that therefore it was the policy of the United States not to pay ransom. He acknowledged that this policy was "heartbreaking" in individual cases but felt that to do otherwise would be to encourage terrorist groups to kidnap Americans.[16]

This policy of "no concessions" was emphatically restated in September 1976 following the hijacking of a TWA airliner from New York to Paris by Croatian nationalists. The terrorists surrendered peacefully in Paris following negotiations with the French authorities and the American ambassador. In the aftermath of the incident the State Department put out a news release in which it stated that the American policy of refusing to make any concessions to terrorist demands "has not changed and will not change."[17]

The policy of the Carter Administration toward terrorism has also been to refuse to make concessions to terrorist blackmail. In testimony before the Senate Committee on Governmental Affairs in January 1978 Secretary of State Cyrus Vance stated: ". . . we have made clear to all that we will reject terrorist blackmail. We have clearly and repeatedly stated our intention to reject demands for ransom or the release of prisoners."[18] A State Department summary of U.S. policy toward terrorism put out in August 1978 declared, "The U.S. will make no concessions to terrorist blackmail."[19]

A single basic assumption underlies American policy in hostage situations: political kidnappings are motivated by the desire of terrorist groups to secure monetary ransoms and/or to release prisoners. Consequently, what is needed to deter these kidnappings is a firm "no concessions" policy. To make concessions to save one life or a few lives would lead to putting many other lives in danger.

There has been a strong and consistent tendency for American policy makers to regard political kidnappings as common crimes. After the death of Daniel Mitrione, Secretary of State Rogers issued a press release in which he stated, "The spread of terrorism, which cloaks common crimes in political fanaticism, must meet with the repudiation of all men of decency and good will everywhere."[20] In his report on foreign policy for the 1970s Nixon referred to terrorism as a "crime" against "international amity and cooperation."[21] In the aftermath of the Munich Olympics incident Secretary of State Rogers issued a statement which denounced the incident and which declared: "Criminal acts against innocent people . . . are not an acceptable method of solving any of the world's problems."[22] After the Khartoum incident Nixon demanded that "the perpetrators of this crime be brought to justice."[23]

This tendency by American policy makers to regard political hostage situations as ordinary crimes leads them to assume that the motive for such political kidnappings is material reward, just as in criminal kidnappings. True, the nature of the material reward may differ somewhat in political kidnappings (for example, criminals rarely want prisoners set free), but basically political and criminal kidnappings have the same end. And because a political kidnapping has as its goal some sort of material reward, the way to deter these kidnappings is to deny any such reward. In terms of the deterrence theory outlined in Chapter 5, in hostage situations the United States has sought to achieve the deterrence formula, C (costs) $+ R$ (risks) $>B$ (benefits), by denying terrorist groups the B of prisoners and ransoms. In the words of Ambassador Macomber:

We've got to have the fortitude not to pay blackmail, and other countries have got to. And eventually, when they don't get any benefits from this thing and the risks get very high, it will end. But we've got to go on for a while.[24]

The validity of this assumption is called into question by two separate sets of data. The first is derived from cross-national comparisons of the policies of Japan, West Germany, and the United States toward hostage situations. All three nations are large, advanced, industrial societies and are linked together by military and political alliances. Hence in the eyes of many terrorists they are parts of the "capitalist-imperialist" network that they wish to destroy. Despite the similarities between these three nations, there have been significant differences in their policies toward hostage situations between the United States, on the one hand, and West Germany and Japan, on the other. There is reason to believe that terrorist groups have been sensitive to such policy variations.

There is a great deal of evidence that terrorist groups "cross-fertilize" each other by trading information about their operations and their history and hence are aware of the successes and failures of various tactics tried against different adversaries. In the past this process of cross-fertilization was usually indirect: groups would learn about each other by reading the accounts written about past and contemporary terrorist campaigns. The following cases illustrate the way in which one group's activities can indirectly influence those of another.

In Palestine the campaign by the Irgun and Lehi against the British was heavily influenced by the example of the IRA's struggle against the British.[25] At his trial before a British mandate court Avshalom Haviv declared that the British should have learned the futility of repressive measures by what had happened in Ireland. He stated that a free Ireland had arisen in spite of the British executions and imprisonings and that the only result of such measures had been to leave behind in Ireland "ineradicable bloodstains and unforgettable memories."[26]

Just as the history, strategy, and tactics of the IRA had been studied and evaluated by the Jewish underground, later insurgent movements also studied the Irgun and Lehi. The struggle of the EOKA in Cyprus was influenced by the Jewish resistance movement.[27] A Tupamaro leader stated in an interview that the struggle of the Jews in Palestine had been closely studied by his movement.[28] And Sean MacStiofain, the chief of staff of the Provisional IRA in 1970-1972, noted in his memoirs that he had carefully read Menachem Begin's book *The Revolt.*[29]

The influence that the Algerian revolution and the Palestinian movements had on the FLQ in Canada is demonstrated by an interview with an FLQ leader in which the leader stated the FLQ was seeking to stage ever more spectacular operations "like the Palestinians" and in which he compared the problems of Quebec with the problems that Algeria had prior to independence.[30]

While this process of indirectly trading information continues, in the past few years cross-fertilization among various revolutionary organizations has also taken place by means of direct person-to-person meetings and encounters. In February 1974 the Uruguayan National Liberation Movement (Tupamaros), the Bolivian National Liberation Army, the Chilean Movement of the Revolutionary Left, and the Argentine People's Revolutionary Army (ERP) announced the formation of a joint revolutionary council to combat imperialism throughout Latin America.[31] George Habash's PFLP has had personal contacts with two similar movements, the Baader-Meinhof group of West Germany[32] and the United Red Army of Japan.[33] On December 20, 1973, thirteen suspected terrorists—ten Turks, two Palestinians, and one Algerian—were arrested in Villiers-Sur-Marne, 48 miles east of Paris.[34] Finally, there is the case of Ilich Ramirez Sanchez, "Carlos." It appears that he was at the center of a network of ties among a number of various terrorist groups, including the United Red Army, the Baader-Meinhof group, the PFLP, and some of the Latin American organizations.[35]

Given this clear evidence that terrorist groups are aware of the successes and failures of each other, there is every reason to believe that they would be sensitive to the policy differences on terrorist incidents among the United States, West Germany, and Japan.

In the period 1970-1975 West Germany and Japan pursued a much more accommodating policy toward hostage situations than did the United States. For example, there was the von Spreti incident. On March 31, 1970, the West German ambassador to Guatemala, Count Karl von Spreti, was kidnapped by a group of Guatemalan terrorists. The West German government put considerable pressure on the Guatemalan authorities to give in to the terrorists' demands, but they refused. Von Spreti was executed. In protest against the Guatemalan government's refusal to accede to the demands of the terrorists, the West Germans withdrew most of their mission staff from Guatemala and asked the Guatemalan ambassador to leave Bonn.[36] This West German policy of trying to accommodate terrorist demands in hostage situations was repeated several times over the next five years. West Germany released three captured Palestinian terrorists as part of a package deal to free the West German and other nationals seized in the September 1970 hijackings by the PFLP.[37] In February 1972 the West German government paid a $5 million ransom to obtain the release of a Lufthansa plane and its passengers and crew that had been hijacked by Palestinian terrorists to Southern Yemen.[38] Any impression of a stiffening of West Germany policy toward hostage situations that may have been indicated by the unsuccessful attempt to rescue the Israeli athletes captured during the Munich Olympics in September 1972 was dissipated six weeks later when the West Germans released the surviving members of the Palestinian squad that had carried out the Munich operation in order to secure the safe return of the crew and passengers of a hijacked Lufthansa jet.[39] Finally, in early March 1975 the West Germans flew five members of the Baader-Meinhof group to Southern Yemen in order to secure the release of Peter Lorenz, the kidnapped Christian Democratic candidate for mayor of West Berlin.[40]

Japan pursued a similar policy toward political kidnappings in this period. On March 11, 1970, Nobuo Okuchi, the Japanese consul in Sao Paulo, Brazil, was kidnapped by Brazilian terrorists.

The Japanese government put pressure on the Brazilian authorities to give in and publicly thanked them when they met the kidnappers demands and flew five prisoners to Mexico.[41] Over the next five years the Japanese several times repeated their policy of accommodating terrorist demands in order to secure the release of hostages. In July 1973 a JAL 747 was hijacked and flown to Dubai. Japanese government officials arrived at Dubai prepared to negotiate; but the hijackers, apparently disoriented because the leader of the group had killed herself accidentally with a grenade during the takeover, rebuffed the officials and flew on to Benghazi, Libya, where they destroyed the aircraft after letting off the passengers and crew.[42] On January 31, 1974, two United Red Army members and two PFLP members took three persons hostage on a ferry boat in Singapore following the failure of an attempt to blow up a Shell oil refinery. On February 6 five PFLP members invaded the Japanese embassy in Kuwait and seized twelve hostages. The PFLP members in Kuwait demanded a plane to fly both themselves and the terrorists in Singapore to a sanctuary. The Japanese government agreed to their demands and flew all the terrorists to Southern Yemen.[43]

Clearly, in the period 1970-1975 the West German and Japanese policies toward hostage incidents were more accommodating than was American policy. The question is, what effect did these more accommodating policies have on the incidence of political kidnapping among the three nations? By the logic of the American assumption that political kidnappings are motivated by the desire to attain rewards of prisoners and money, there should have been more hostage situations involving West German and Japanese nationals. After all, if prisoners and money are what the terrorists are after, it made no sense to kidnap an American, because the United States would not make any effort to accommodate those demands, while the West Germans and the Japanese would go to considerable lengths to meet demands and would pressure other governments to do so as well.

To test the assumption that underlies American policy, three separate time frames for the years 1970-1975 have been set up for the United States, West Germany, and Japan. The time frames were five-year periods running from a date in 1970 on which the policy of the country in question toward political kidnappings was widely publicized. For Japan the time frame runs from March 12, 1970, to March 11, 1975, with the beginning date the day after the kidnapping of Okuchi, the Japanese consul in Sao Paulo, Brazil. For West Germany the time frame runs from April 1, 1970, to March 31, 1975, with the beginning date the day after the kidnapping of von Spreti, the West German ambassador to Guatemala. For the United States the time frame runs from August 11, 1970, to August 10, 1975, with the beginning date the day after the body of Agency for International Development adviser Mitrione was found in Montevideo, Uruguay. Next, three separate data sources have been reviewed for instances of political kidnappings: Jenkins and Johnson's *International Terrorism: A Chronology, 1968-1974*, a series of chronologies from the office of the special assistant to the Secretary of State for combatting terrorism, and the *New York Times* index on the various countries. The incidents from these three sources have been recorded in Table IV.

For a hostage situation to be included in the table three conditions had to be met. First a national of the United States, Japan, or West Germany had to be involved and to have been deliberately targeted; situations where such nationals were not deliberately targeted but rather were part of a larger group of hostages, as is the case with many hijackings, were excluded. Second, the kidnappings had to be by a politically motivated group; purely criminal cases were excluded. And third, the hostage situation had to have some international significance; purely domestic kidnappings were excluded. "International significance" has any of the following characteristics: the nationals of one country were seized while overseas; the hostage situation took place at home but the abductors were foreign; the hostage situation, wherever it took place, involved flying people from one country to another.

Table IV lists both the total number of hostage incidents and the subset of these incidents which involved ransom demands being made on companies and individuals. This breakdown of what are called "private kidnappings" is provided because such kidnappings are somewhat different from the rest of the hostage situations in that in other hostage situations the incident was intended directly or indirectly to have an impact on a government.

The logic of the assumption behind American policy toward hostage situations would argue that there should have been more

TABLE IV. *Political Hostage Situations Involving West German,
Japanese, and American Nationals*

	NUMBER OF INCIDENTS
Political hostage situations involving West German nationals from April 1, 1970, to March 31, 1975	
Total hostage incidents	12
Private kidnappings	2
Political hostage situations involving Japanese nationals from March 12, 1970, to March 11, 1975	
Total hostage incidents	3
Private kidnappings	0
Political hostage situations involving American nationals from August 11, 1970, to August 10, 1975	
Total hostage incidents	34
Private kidnappings	13

kidnappings involving West German and Japanese than Americans since these countries have been considerably more willing to accommodate terrorist demands for prisoners and ransoms. Yet the data from Table IV clearly reveals that this has not been the case, and hence the validity of this assumption is called into question.

The comparative analysis undertaken above could be challenged on the following grounds: such cross-national comparisons are misleading because there are too many variables that these comparisons do not take into account. In other words, the United States, West Germany, and Japan are just too different in size, in political history, and in their position in world politics to be compared concerning their policies on international terrorism.

The proper response to this objection should make two points. First, while there are a number of differences between the United States, West Germany, and Japan, there are also a number of important similarities; all three of these nations are large advanced industrial societies, all three of them are part of the Western alliance system, and because they are advanced industrial societies and are part of the Western alliances all three of them are seen by many terrorists as part of the "capitalist-imperialist" network they seek to destroy. Second, it is not being claimed that this comparative analysis totally refutes the assumptions behind American policy toward diplomatic kidnappings. What *is* being argued is that the results of this comparative analysis are at odds with what the logic behind U.S. policy indicates that the results should be and are at odds to such a degree that this logic must be seriously questioned.

Table IV points out another fact that casts doubts upon the validity of the American assumption that political kidnappings are motivated by the desire for material rewards, namely, American nationals continue to be seized despite the widespread publicity that the American "no concessions" policy has achieved. Several high officials charged with carrying out American policy toward hostage situations indicated in interviews that there is substantial evidence that terrorist groups are well aware of American policy—so aware that frequently groups holding American hostages do not even make demands for prisoners and ransoms.[44] But if terrorists accept the fact that the United States will not accommodate their demands for money and prisoners, why is it that an August 1978 CIA study on terrorism found that of the political hostage situations in the seven-year period 1971-1977 a heavily disproportionate number (35 percent) involved American nationals?[45]

The explanation for why there have been significantly more hostage situations involving the United States than West Germany or Japan and for why American nationals continue to be kidnapped despite the widespread publicity its "no concessions" policy has received is that a group undertaking a campaign of terrorism has five possible tactical goals, only one of which is the securing of funds and the release of prisoners. And while it may make more sense to kidnap a national from some country other than the United States if one's goals are prisoners and money, *kidnapping an American national will frequently be more likely to lead to the attainment of one or more of the other four goals.*

In addition to the goal of prisoners and ransoms, Chapter 3 listed four other tactical goals of a terrorist campaign: (a) publicity, (b) the polarization of society, (c) disruption of state-to-state relations, and (d) harassment of the authorities. Looking first at the goal of publicity, given the importance of the United States in world politics, if a group wants publicity it makes much more sense to kidnap an American national, especially an important American national like an ambassador, than a national or an ambassador of a smaller and less important country. As American Ambassador to Brazil Elbrick stated when questioned about the motives of his kidnappers: "My abductors told me that they took me because no one would have cared if they had taken the Turkish ambassador."[46]

If a terrorist group is seeking to force governmental repression so as to polarize society, then here again the kidnapping of an American national, given the large role that the United States plays in the domestic and foreign affairs of many countries, makes much more sense than the kidnapping of a national of a state that plays only a minor role in the internal and external affairs of the country where the terrorist group is operating. Carlos Marighella, a Brazilian theorist of urban guerrilla warfare, insisted on the need to force governmental repression so as to speed up revolutionary change.[47] This theory of Marighella's leads one to conclude that the Brazilian terrorists who kidnapped Elbrick had more than publicity in mind when they told him that no one would have cared if they had seized the Turkish ambassador: the kidnapping of the Turkish ambassador also would have been much less likely to goad the Brazilian authorities into repressive acts.

As for the third potential goal of a terrorist campaign, that of disrupting state-to-state relations, once again there are compelling reasons for an American target. The United States, as one of the two superpowers, plays an important role in virtually every region of the world. Hence, if one wants to raise tensions in a particular region, kidnapping and/or killing Americans makes a great deal of sense while attacks on nationals of countries that play only a minor role in the region make no sense. Thus when the radicals in the Palestinian movement sought to disrupt first the Rogers peace plan of 1970 and then the Geneva Conference of early 1974 it was hardly accidental that Americans were among their victims in the Dawson field incident of September 1970 and the Rome airport incident of December 1973.[48]

Finally, a terrorist group seeking to harass and demoralize the authorities and their security apparatus will frequently find it expedient to attack Americans because the United States provides training and advisers to the government side in many contemporary insurgencies. So if one wants to weaken the government's authority and its ability to control the country, it makes sense to kidnap and/or assassinate American military and police advisers serving in foreign nations. The assassination of two American military officers in Guatemala in January 1968 and the kidnapping and subsequent execution in July and August of 1970 of Daniel Mitrione in Uruguay are cases in point.[49]

In conclusion, the claim by American officials that a policy of refusing all concessions to terrorists holding Americans hostage will deter such hostage incidents is of questionable accuracy. In contrast, the costs of such a policy, in the form of lessening the chances that an American national will survive a political kidnapping, are very real. In neither the governmental nor private hostage situations involving West German or Japanese nationals listed in Table IV were any of the nationals killed. In contrast, in the twenty-one American governmental hostage situations listed in Table IV, there were a total of five American hostages killed, an average of 0.23 fatalities per situation. The number of American deaths almost certainly would have been higher were it not for the fact that in eleven of the thirteen American private political kidnappings listed in Table IV the demands of the terrorists were totally met. (In the twelfth instance the company involved tried to pay a ransom, but the local government seized the money. Whether or not a ransom was paid in the thirteenth case is not known.) In light of the questionable benefits and real costs of the current American policy toward hostage situations, there is a need to undertake a fundamental reformulation of this policy.

NOTES

1. *New York Times*, September 6, 1969.
2. *New York Times*, September 8, 1969.
3. Interview No. 33 (Sean Holly).
4. Interview No. 32 (Staff Member of the Office of the Special Assistant to the Secretary of State for Combatting Terrorism).

5. Carol Baumann, *The Diplomatic Kidnappings* (The Hague: Martinus Nijhoff, 1973), p. 107.

6. Brian M. Jenkins and Janera Johnson, *International Terrorism: A Chronology, 1968-1974* (Santa Monica, California: The RAND Corporation, R-1597-DOS/ARPA, 1975), p. 23.

7. Henry Brandon, *The Retreat of American Power* (Garden City, New York: Doubleday & Company, Inc., 1973), p. 129.

8. J. Bowyer Bell, *Transnational Terror* (Washington, D.C.: American Enterprise Institute, 1975), p. 61.

9. Richard Nixon, "U.S. Foreign Policy for the 1970's: Building for Peace," *Department of State Bulletin*, March 22, 1971, p. 426.

10. Interview No. 23 (Robert Myers).

11. Jenkins and Johnson, *Terrorism Chronology*, p. 39.

12. "Deputy Under Secretary Macomber Discusses Terrorism on 'Today' Program," *Department of State Bulletin*, April 2, 1973, p. 400.

13. "Remarks by President Nixon, March 6, 1973," *Department of State Bulletin*, March 26, 1973, p. 350.

14. "Terrorism, Part 2," hearings before the Committee on Internal Security, House of Representatives, 93rd Congress, 2nd Session (May 8, 14, 16, 22, 29, and 30, and June 13, 1974), pp. 3136-3137.

15. Interview No. 25 (Allison Palmer).

16. "Secretary Kissinger's News Conference at Vail, Colorado, August 17, 1975," *Department of State Bulletin*, September 15, 1975, p. 408; "Secretary Kissinger Appears Before Southern Governors Conference," *Department of State Bulletin*, October 6,1975, p. 527.

17. "Policy of Refusal to Negotiate with Terrorists Reiterated," *Department of State Bulletin*, October 11, 1976, p. 453.

18. "Terrorism: Scope of the Threat and Need for Effective Legislation," *Department of State Bulletin*, March 1978, p. 54.

19. "Terrorism," Bureau of Public Affairs, Department of State, August 1978.

20. "Statement by Secretary Rogers, August 10, 1970," *Department of State Bulletin*, August 31, 1970, p. 247.

21. Nixon, "U.S. Foreign Policy for the 1970's," p. 426.

22. "Statement by Secretary Rogers (Press Release Dated September 6, 1972)," *Department of State Bulletin*, October 2, 1972, p. 360.

23. "Statement by President Nixon," *Department of State Bulletin*, March 26, 1973, p. 353.

24. "Deputy Under Secretary Macomber Discusses Terrorism on 'Today' Program," p. 401.

25. Interviews No. 7 (Nathan Yalin-Mor) and No. 8 (Eli Tavin).

26. Menachem Begin, *The Revolt* (Jerusalem: Steimatzky's Agency Limited, 1972), p. 284.

27. Interview No. 8 (Eli Tavin).

28. "Interview with 'Urbano' (Tupamaro Leader) by Leopoldo Madruga," in *Urban Guerrilla Warfare in Latin America*, ed. James Kohl and John Litt (Cambridge, Massachusetts: The M.I.T. Press, 1974), p. 285.

29. Sean MacStiofain, *Revolutionary in Ireland* (Edinburgh, Scotland: R & R Clark, Ltd., 1975), p. 41.

30. John Saywell, *Quebec 70* (Toronto: University of Toronto Press, 1970), p. 134.

31. *New York Times*, February 15, 1974.

32. Interview No. 4 (Rehoboam Ze'ev).

33. Jenkins and Johnson, *Terrorism Chronology*, pp. 32-33 and 53.

34. Bell, *Transnational Terror*, p. 71.

35. Robert Fisk, "The World's Terrorists Sometimes Are United," *New York Times*, August 17, 1975.

36. Baumann, *Diplomatic Kidnappings*, pp. 96-100.

37. Bell, *Transnational Terror*, p. 61.

38. Jenkins and Johnson, *Terrorism Chronology*, p. 31.

39. Ibid., p. 35.

40. *New York Times*, March 5, 1975.

41. *New York Times*, March 16, 1970.

42. Jenkins and Johnson, *Terrorism Chronology*, p. 46.

43. Ibid., p. 53.

44. Interviews No. 23 (Robert Myers) and No. 26 (Robert Feary).

45. *International Terrorism in 1977*, Central Intelligence Agency, August 1978, p. 11.

46. "Terrorism, Part 2," hearings before the Committee on Internal Security, House of Representatives, 93rd Congress, 2nd Session (May 8, 14, 16, 22, 29, and 30, and June 13, 1974), p. 3129.

47. Carlos Marighella, "The Minimanual of the Urban Guerrilla," appendix in Robert Moss, *Urban Guerrilla Warfare* (London: International Institute for Strategic Studies, 1971), p. 40.

48. William B. Quandt, Fuad Jabber, and Ann Mosely Lesch, *The Politics of Palestinian Nationalism* (Berkeley, California: University of California Press, 1973), p. 125; *New York Times*, December 18, 1973.

49. Jenkins and Johnson, *Terrorism Chronology*, pp. 12, 23.

chapter 7

AMERICAN EFFORTS TO ATTAIN MULTILATERAL DETERRENCE

With the resurgence of terrorism in the late 1960s, American officials became concerned that transnational terrorism was being encouraged by the ability of terrorists to escape being punished for their acts.[1] Terrorists would stage an incident in one country and then seek sanctuary in another. When such incidents did not involve the taking of hostages, the American "no concessions" policy was irrelevant as a deterrent, and so in recent years the United States has pushed for a number of multilateral conventions against international terrorism. The rationale for these conventions was that they would strengthen deterrence of terrorist acts by raising the costs and risks of undertaking them.

The United States vigorously supported the three anti-hijacking accords (Tokyo, 1963; The Hague, 1970; and Montreal, 1971) and has attempted to put teeth into these treaties by trying to get an international agreement to apply sanctions to any country that provides safe havens to hijackers.[2] In addition to supporting anti-hijacking conventions, the United States has backed two treaties designed to protect diplomats from attacks by terrorists. First, there is the "Convention to Prevent and Punish Acts of Terrorism Taking the Form of Crimes Against Persons and Related Extortion that Are of International Significance." This convention was adopted by the Organization of American States General Assembly in February 1971. It was open for signature to all states, but basically the thrust of the convention was to deter acts of terrorism against diplomats and diplomatic agents in the Americas. The treaty pledged its signatories to either extradite or punish any individual who committed an act of terrorism as defined by the convention.[3] The treaty entered into effect in October 1973.[4] The second diplomats' convention is the "Convention on the Prevention and Punishment of Crimes Against Diplomatic Agents and Other Internationally Protected Persons," which was adopted by the General Assembly of the United Nations in December 1973. This convention was the culmination of several years of work by the International Law Commission. Its scope is limited, as the title indicates, to the protection of diplomatic personnel. The convention obligates all signatory states to either extradite or punish anyone within their national borders who is guilty of an offense under its provisions.[5] The convention came into force in February 1977.[6]

While both of these conventions have some points of interest, they are so narrowly construed (i.e., their scope is restricted to diplomatic agents and diplomats) that they do not in any sense constitute a general network of deterrence against international terrorism. Since this book is discussing American efforts to deter terrorist acts against all of its nationals, this chapter will focus on the major American effort to deter such acts, namely, the "Draft Convention on Terrorism" which the United States introduced in the United Nations in September 1972. (For the text of this convention see Appendix III.)

This draft convention defined a terrorist as "any person who unlawfully kills, causes serious bodily harm or kidnaps another person, attempts to commit such an act, or participates as an accomplice of a person who commits or attempts to commit any such act."[7] The convention thus protected all individuals, not just diplomats. The convention was strictly limited to terrorist acts of "international significance." International significance was defined as having the following components:

A. Is committed or takes effect outside the territory of a state of which the alleged offender is a national.
B. Is committed or takes effect (a) outside the territory of the state against which the act is directed or (b) within the territory of the state against

which the act is directed and the alleged offender knows or has reason to know that a person against whom the act is directed is not a national of that state.

C. Is committed neither by nor against a member of the armed forces of a state in the course of military hostilities.

D. Is intended to damage the interest of or obtain concessions from a state or an international organization.[8]

Even with these fairly precise guidelines, exactly what acts would be covered by the convention was open to dispute. However, the United States went to considerable lengths to reassure any and all concerned that the convention did not cover purely internal conflicts and did not deny the right of national self-determination. John R. Stevenson, a legal adviser to the American United Nations delegation, stated in a speech that the convention would not deal with internal conflicts unless such conflicts were exported to the territory of third states or were directed against third-country nationals. He further stated that the United States was a strong defender of the right of national self-determination and that the convention it had proposed would not affect this right in any way.[9]

The key provision of the American draft convention was Article 3, which pledged each of the signatories to either extradite or punish any individual on its territory who was guilty of a terrorist act of international significance:

A state party in whose territory an alleged offender is found shall, if it does not extradite him, submit, without exception whatsoever and without undue delay, the case to its competent authorities for the purpose of prosecution, through proceedings in accordance with the laws of that state.[10]

The American draft convention was introduced into the United Nations General Assembly by Secretary of State Rogers in a speech on September 25, 1972. Rogers' speech was in direct response to Secretary General Waldheim's decision to put the item of international terrorism on the agenda of the United Nations. Waldheim had so acted because of the wave of international concern about terrorism that had been generated by the Munich Olympics incident in early September 1972. The legal advisers to the American delegation to the United Nations had drawn up the convention in response to Waldheim's action.[11] Along with the draft convention the United States introduced a resolution which called upon all states to become parties to the three existing anti-hijacking treaties; requested the International Civil Aviation Organization to urgently pursue the drafting of a convention to enforce the Tokyo, Hague, and Montreal conventions; and demanded the convening of a conference in early 1973 to adopt a convention on the prevention and punishment of international terrorism, for which purpose the American draft convention could serve as a basis for discussion.[12]

In pushing for its convention, the United States made essentially two arguments. The first was that action against terrorism was imperative in order to protect the lives of innocent people. As Secretary Rogers said in his speech to the General Assembly in introducing the draft convention:

> The issue is not war—war between states, civil war, or revolutionary war. The issue is not the striving of people to achieve self-determination and independence.
>
> Rather, it is whether millions of air travelers can continue to fly in safety each year. It is whether a person who receives a letter can open it without the fear of being blown up. It is whether international meetings—like the Olympic games, like this assembly—can proceed without the ever-present threat of violence.
>
> We all recognize that issues such as self-determination must continue to be addressed seriously by the international community. But political passion, however deeply held, cannot be a justification for criminal violence against innocent people.[13]

The second argument used by the United States in support of the draft convention was that terrorism posed a serious threat to international order. In a speech to the Sixth Committee (where the convention was debated), W. Tapley Bennett, the chief U.S. delegate to the committee, stated that the current "epidemic of violence" was threatening "the very fabric of international order and the most fundamental of rights."[14]

These American arguments about the preservation of innocent lives and the protection of international order were echoed by other states in the debates in the Sixth Committee. With regard to the issue of the preservation of innocent life, the delegate from The Netherlands stated:

The community of nations could no longer tolerate acts of terrorism. In one way or another, it would have to counter that evil if the lives of increasing numbers of innocent bystanders were not to be endangered.[15]

Concerning the issue of the protection of international order, the delegate from Uruguay argued:

However, for those who believed that terrorism could be justified for certain motives, it should be pointed out that all terrorism was met by terrorism, so that jungle law would reign, no one would be safe, and retaliation would replace the principles of the charter.[16]

The American draft convention and resolution immediately ran into strong opposition from a coalition of Arab, Asian, African, and communist states. These states' central objection was that action against international terrorism could potentially interfere with wars of national liberation. This objection took three separate forms. The first was that racist and colonialist powers could exploit the issue of international terrorism to justify their oppression. The delegate from Senegal stated:

An attempt was being made to raise the spectre of international terrorism as a pretext for calling for severe measures and sanctions against all who were seeking to make radical changes in the order established by a minority of racist and colonialist opportunists.[17]

The second form of this objection concerning wars of national liberation was that colonial and racist regimes were terroristic, but the actions of such regimes were dealt with neither by the convention introduced by the United States nor by its resolution. The delegate from Libya argued:

The definition (of terrorism) must cover not only acts committed by persons for criminal purposes but also every act committed by criminal colonizers or oppressors against peace-loving peoples, and every act which prevented peoples from exercising their legitimate activities or deprived them of their inalienable right to their homeland.[18]

The third form of the objection concerning wars of national liberation was that the problem of international terrorism was not really very important and that this so-called problem distracted the attention of the community of nations from the real issues of imperialistic aggression, racism, and colonialism. The delegate from Egypt declared:

Oppression, repression, segregation and subjugation were mere synonyms for colonialism, racial discrimination, *apartheid* and military occupation. These were the real problems, and in the opinion of his delegation they merited the highest priority in treatment by the United Nations. . . . Instead of magnifying beyond proportion the desperate acts of a small minority of oppressed people, the international community should be appalled when Africans and Asians were the victims of another form of terrorism, perpetrated with the aid of modern technology.[19]

As Table V shows, of the 76 nations that voted down the American-backed initiatives against international terrorism, some 57 made speeches during the debates in the Sixth Committee. Of these 57, a total of 53 directly mentioned the question of international terrorism and wars of national liberation. In their speeches these nations raised in one or more of its three forms the objection that action against terrorism might interfere with wars of national liberation.[20]

Table V also records three other reservations that were raised with respect to the American efforts against transnational terrorism. It was argued, first, that it was necessary to study the causes of terrorism; second, that definitions were unclear; and third, that the United Nations was being asked to act in haste. A closer examination of these three objections, however, indicates that fundamentally they all led back to the issue of wars of national liberation.

Looking first at the objection that the causes of terrorism were not being studied, these causes were usually held to be racism, colonialism, and foreign occupation. The delegate from Syria stated:

The underlying causes of all forms of terrorism and other acts of violence were colonialism and foreign domination, denial of the right to self-determination . . .[21]

The objection that definitions were unclear centered around concern that terrorism and wars of national liberation might be confused. The delegate from India voiced this concern:

. . . great care must be taken to ensure that the offense was so defined as not to affect the exercise of the right to self-determination and the legitimacy of the struggle against colonial and racist regimes and all forms of foreign domination.[22]

Finally, the objection that the United Nations was being asked to act in haste was linked to the argument that it was necessary to study the causes of terrorism which, as was noted above, were held to be racism, colonialism, and foreign domination. The delegate from Tunisia declared:

His delegation was, moreover, opposed to the idea of being led, through global condemnations, to the hasty adoption of texts dealing with terrorism in general, and it did not understand why certain delegations were not equally eager to adopt effective decisions when it came to the question of the causes of international terrorism.[23]

The United States made two arguments in reply to the objections of this coalition of Third World and communist countries. First, it stated that even just struggles, such as those for national liberation, did not justify immoral means such as the taking of innocent lives.[24] Second, the United States maintained that action on the problem of terrorism could not await a study of its causes. Ambassador W. Tapley Bennett stated that the elimination of the causes of terrorism would take a long time and that it was wrong to do nothing while waiting for these causes to be eliminated. He noted that people did not refuse medical care simply because all of the causes of their disease were not known and that nations did not hesitate to prohibit murder even though the injustices that produced violence had not been fully identified or eliminated.[25]

These arguments that even just causes do not justify immoral methods and that delay on the question of terrorism was not acceptable were echoed by other states. The delegate from Denmark stated that "even in time of war" certain forms of violence, "especially against the innocent," were to be considered illegitimate.[26] The delegate from Iceland declared that it was necessary to study the causes of terrorism but that "the search for a solution could not await the rectification of injustices."[27]

The American delegation to the Sixth Committee, realizing that its resolution commanded little support, switched its support to a resolution introduced by a group composed mostly of West European and Latin American states. This resolution, like the American resolution, called for prompt international action against terrorism, including the drafting of an international convention and the strengthening of existing anti-hijacking measures, but unlike the American resolution it had a paragraph reaffirming the right of national self-determination.[28] It was hoped by the American delegation that this second resolution would meet the objections raised by the coalition of Third World and communist countries to the American resolution.[29] This second resolution also failed to meet these objections, and instead this coalition of states opposed to the American initiatives introduced and passed a resolution of its own. This third resolution called for no immediate international measures and instead referred all action on terrorism to an ad hoc committee to meet in 1973.[30] (The texts of all three of these resolutions are in Appendix III.) The ad hoc committee did meet for several weeks in 1973 but was unable to come to any agreement on the problem of terrorism.[31] As had apparently been the intention of the coalition of states that passed the resolution, referring the issue to a special committee effectively killed the chances for any steps against international terrorism.[32]

Tables V,[33] VI,[34] and VII[35] summarize the Sixth Committee debates in the fall of 1972. Table V is a content analysis of the speeches of the states that opposed the American efforts to take action against terrorism. The incidence of four specific themes that recurred in these speeches is recorded: (a) action against terrorism must not be allowed to interfere with national liberation struggles, (b) the definitions involved in the problem of international terrorism were unclear, (c) the causes of terrorism must be studied as well as its remedies, and (d) the United Nations was being asked to act in haste.

Table VI is a content analysis of the speeches made by states that supported measures against international terrorism. The incidence of four themes that were in a number of these addresses is recorded: (a) innocent lives must be protected, (b) international order must be defended, (c) just causes do not excuse immoral methods, and (d) delay in taking steps against terrorism pending study of the causes of terrorism is not warranted. Finally, Table VII records the vote on the Third World and communist bloc resolution that was finally passed by the Sixth Committee over the objections of the United States and its supporters. These American objections were summed up by Ambassador Bennett: ". . . that text made a political issue out of what was, in his delegation's view, a human one . . ."[36]

The fundamental reason why the American-backed initiatives did not make any headway in the United Nations in the fall of 1972 was that those handling the American policy efforts failed to understand that to a large majority of states in the United Nations terrorism was perceived as a political rather than a humanitarian issue. A humanitarian issue is one on which there is a broad consensus that the phenomenon in question is a problem, and the only disagreements are over technical questions about how best to deal with the problem. A political issue, on the other hand, is one on which there is no agreement that the phenomenon in question is a problem. Consequently the disagreements that arise are over basic values rather than technical questions.

The international relief effort that was launched to aid the victims of the large earthquake in Nicaragua in 1972 is a classic illustration of a humanitarian issue. There were disagreements concerning the relief effort over which nations should supply what and over how the aid should be administered, but there was no disagreement about the fact that the earthquake had generated an international problem that had to be dealt with. The issue of Soviet arms shipments to the Arab states, on the other hand, is a political issue: there is no international consensus that such shipments are a problem, and consequently the disagreements that take place concerning these shipments reflect value conflicts rather than technical differences. To be sure, the humanitarian versus political distinction outlined here is more like a continuum than a set of sharp and clear categories into which issues can be placed. The point is that a large number of issues are very close to either the "humanitarian pole" of the continuum or to the "political pole" of the continuum and that most other issues are closer to one pole than to the other.

To the American officials charged with trying to get international action against terrorism, terrorism was clearly perceived as a humanitarian issue. They said as much in their speeches, and the arguments they used in support of their efforts were humanitarian in nature.

TABLE V.   *The Arguments of the States Opposed*
            to Action Against Terrorism

	LIBERATION STRUGGLES	DEFINITIONS UNCLEAR	CAUSES MUST BE STUDIED	ACTING IN HASTE
Albania	X			
Algeria	X			
Beylorussian SSR	X	X		
Bulgaria	X			
Burundi	X		X	
Cameroon	X	X	X	
Chad	X			
China	X			
Cuba	X			
Cyprus	X		X	
Czechoslovakia	X			
Democratic Yemen	X		X	
Ecuador	X			
Egypt	X	X	X	
Ghana	X			X
Guinea	X		X	
Guyana	X			
Hungary	X			
India	X			X
Indonesia	X		X	
Iraq	X	X		X
Jamaica	X		X	X
Jordan	X	X		X
Kuwait	X			X
Lebanon	X		X	
Liberia			X	
Libya	X	X		X
Madagascar	X	X		X
Malaysia			X	
Mali	X		X	

TABLE V. (Cont.)

	LIBERATION STRUGGLES	DEFINITIONS UNCLEAR	CAUSES MUST BE STUDIED	ACTING IN HASTE
Mauritania	X		X	
Mexico			X	
Mongolia	X		X	
Niger	X	X		
Nigeria			X	
Oman	X			
Pakistan	X		X	
Peru	X			X
Poland	X		X	
Roumania	X			
Saudi Arabia	X		X	X
Senegal	X	X	X	X
Sierra Leone	X			
Somalia	X	X	X	X
Sri Lanka	X	X		
Sudan	X		X	X
Syria	X		X	
Tanzania	X	X	X	X
Tunisia	X		X	X
UAE	X		X	
Uganda	X	X		
Ukrainian SSR	X			
USSR	X			
Venezuela	X	X	X	
Yemen	X	X	X	
Yugoslavia	X			
Zambia	X			
57 countries	53	15	28	15

TABLE VI.   *The Arguments of the States in Favor of Action Against Terrorism*

	PROTECTION OF INNOCENT LIVES	DEFENSE OF INTERNATIONAL ORDER	IMMORAL METHODS	DELAY NOT JUSTIFIED
Australia			X	X
Austria	X	X	X	X
Belgium	X	X		X
Bolivia	X			
Brazil	X			
Canada	X			
Colombia			X	
Costa Rica	X	X		
Denmark	X		X	X
Dominican Republic				
Fiji Islands	X			
Guatemala				
Haiti		X		
Iceland	X	X	X	X
Iran	X	X	X	X
Israel	X			
Italy	X	X		X
Japan	X			
Lesotho	X			
The Netherlands	X			X
New Zealand			X	X
Nicaragua	X	X	X	
Paraguay	X			X
Philippines				
Portugal				
South Africa	X			
Turkey		X		X
United Kingdom	X	X	X	X
United States	X	X	X	X
Uruguay	X	X	X	X
30 countries	21	12	11	14

TABLE VII.   *The Vote on the Resolution Referring Action on Terrorism to an Ad Hoc Committee*

In favor: Afghanistan, Albania, Algeria, Bahrain, Beylorussian SSR, Botswana, Bulgaria, Burma, Burundi, Cameroon, Central African Republic, Chad, Chile, China, Congo, Cyprus, Czechoslovakia, Dahomey, Democratic Yemen, Ecuador, Egypt, Equatorial Guinea, Ethiopia, Gabon, Gambia, Ghana, Guinea, Guyana, Hungary, India, Indonesia, Iraq, Jamaica, Jordan, Kenya, Kuwait, Lebanon, Liberia, Libya, Madagascar, Malaysia, Mali, Mauritania, Mexico, Mongolia, Morocco, Niger, Nigeria, Oman, Pakistan, Panama, Peru, Poland, Qatar, Roumania, Rwanda, Saudi Arabia, Senegal, Sierra Leone, Somalia, Sri Lanka, Sudan, Syria, Togo, Trinidad and Tobago, Tunisia, Uganda, Ukrainian SSR, United Arab Emirates, United Republic of Tanzania, Upper Volta, USSR, Venezuela, Yemen, Yugoslavia, Zambia (76)

In opposition: Australia, Austria, Belgium, Bolivia, Brazil, Canada, Colombia, Costa Rica, Cuba,* Denmark, Dominican Republic, Fiji Islands, Guatemala, Haiti, Honduras, Iceland, Iran, Israel, Italy, Japan, Laos, Lesotho, Luxembourg, The Netherlands, New Zealand, Nicaragua, Paraguay, Philippines, Portugal, South Africa, Turkey, United Kingdom, United States, Uruguay (34)

Abstaining: Argentina, Barbados, El Salvador, Finland, France, Greece, Ireland, Ivory Coast, Malawi, Nepal, Norway, Singapore, Spain, Sweden, Thailand, Zaire (16)

*Cuba voted against the resolution not because it wanted immediate steps against terrorism but because it opposed the whole idea of discussing terrorism. The Cuban representative said that such discussions were an attempt to stifle wars of national liberation.

W. Tapley Bennett, American representative to the Sixth Committee

He recalled that the United States Secretary of State, addressing the General Assembly, had said that the issue was not an issue of war, whether between states, civil war, or revolutionary war, and was not the striving of people to achieve self-determination and independence. Rather, it was whether millions of air travelers could continue to fly in safety each year, whether a person could open his mail without fear of being blown up, whether diplomats could carry out their duties safely and whether international meetings could proceed without the ever-present threat of violence. *It was not an issue which should divide the international community. It was a human problem.*[37]

John R. Stevenson, legal adviser to the American United Nations delegation

The topic [of international terrorism] has significant political overtones; but the international legal initiatives the U.S. government has taken in the area have been based on what we consider the humanitarian and economic interests of all nations, and we have sought to avoid political complications in meeting a common danger.[38]

Ambassador Bennett repeated his view that terrorism was a humanitarian issue in an article written in 1973:

Recognizing the strong political overtones which accompany the problem of terrorism in many areas of the world, the United States has sought to avoid the political, and to stress the legal and humanitarian, interests of all nations in its proposals. Unfortunately, it must be admitted that we have not been notably successful in our efforts to divorce action on international terrorism from political considerations.[39]

When the American draft convention and resolution were introduced, the American diplomats at the United Nations made two arguments in support of these initiatives: there was a need to protect innocent lives, and international order must be defended. Such arguments are clearly "humanitarian." Unless one is a psychopath, the slaughter of the innocent will be considered a tragedy, and unless one is a hard-core nihilist, the prospect of international chaos is not appealing. In other words, there is a broad international consensus on the need to avoid killing the innocent and on the need to prevent international anarchy, and so by stressing these consensual themes the United States was treating terrorism as a humanitarian problem.

The reason why the American initiatives against terrorism failed to get anywhere in the United Nations was that a large majority of the nations belonging to that organization did not believe that terrorism was a problem. On the contrary, these nations believed that the really important issue was not terrorism but rather wars of national liberation against racism, colonialism, and *apartheid*. The humanitarian themes pushed by the United States with respect to terrorism were simply ignored by the Third World and communist states because what concerned them was Portuguese Africa, South Africa, Rhodesia, and Israel. The United States posited an international consensus on terrorism as a problem that simply does not exist. As Chapter 2 noted in its discussion of the "ecology of terrorism" and as Chapter 4 showed in its analysis of "surrogate warfare," there are a large number of nations which are either indifferent to international terrorism or seek to exploit the activities of terrorist groups.

In conclusion, reference might be made briefly to an earlier attempt to negotiate a multilateral accord against international terrorism. In 1937 a conference sponsored by the League of Nations drew up a "Convention on the Repression of Terrorism." This convention was the culmination of three years of work in the League of Nations following the assassination in 1934 of Premier Louis Barthou of France and King Alexander of Yugoslavia (the two heads of state were riding in a motorcade in Marseilles at the time of the assassination). Since this convention never received enough ratifications to come into effect, it is now of historical interest only.

The League convention sought to achieve deterrence by providing that the contracting parties agree to either extradite or punish any individual guilty of a terroristic act.[40] An act of terrorism was defined by the convention as follows:

Article I. Acts of terrorism within the meaning of the present convention are criminal acts which are intended or calculated to create a state of terror among individuals, groups of persons, or the general public.[41]

The interesting aspects of the 1937 convention are not its specific articles but rather the arguments that were advanced in favor of

such a convention and the reasons why the convention never received enough ratifications to come into force. The following
quotations are from speeches given at the 1937 conference that
adopted the League convention:

The opening speech of Count Carton De Wiart, president of the conference

. . . we cannot but realize with shame and disgust how advancing knowledge
and improved communications have served in their turn to menace the
security of persons and property and help to promote acts designated by
that new term "terrorism"—acts which, by reason of their gravity and
contagious nature, are prejudicial not only to the interests of individuals as
such or to one or more specific states, but may affect mankind as a whole.[42]

Speech by M. Koukal, a delegate from Czechoslovakia

The Czechoslovak Government had at once realized that the principle
underlying those proposals (against terrorism) was the protection of the
common heritage of the whole civilized world—security of life and limb,
health, liberty and public property intended for the common use—against
the criminal activities of certain terrorists.[43]

Speech by M. Pella, a Roumanian delegate and the conference rapporteur

While, in principle, the value of such arguments (on the non-collaboration
of states in the repression of political offenses) could not be disputed, M.
Pella did not think that they could justify the absolute principle of the
non-collaboration of other countries in repressing offenses which, owing
to their nature, did not merely endanger the order of a given state but social
order in general.[44]

Despite certain differences in language, one can see in these quotations the same two arguments that the United States was to use in
1972 in advancing its convention: that terrorism was a threat to
innocent lives (De Wiart's phrase was "security of persons," while
Koukal's was "security of life") and that terrorism was a danger to
international order (De Wiart said terrorist acts "may affect mankind as a whole," while Pella said terrorism endangered "social

order in general"). In sum, those pushing for multilateral action against terrorism in 1937 made use of the same sort of consensual, humanitarian themes that were used by the proponents of such action in 1972.

The 1937 convention failed to receive enough ratifications to come into force for very much the same set of reasons that the 1972 convention made no headway. That is, in 1937 as in 1972 there was no consensus that terrorism was a serious international problem, and consequently attempts to get action taken against terrorism by treating it as if such a consensus existed were doomed from the outset. The drafters of the 1937 convention called for quite drastic action against international terrorism: persons guilty of terrorist offenses were to be either punished or extradited regardless of whether their acts were politically motivated, propaganda by individuals or groups designed to incite terrorist offenses against other nations were outlawed, and states were to establish strict controls and restrictions on the movement of people across their borders. Such far-reaching steps were unacceptable to most states.[45] At the 1937 conference Sir John Fischer Williams, a delegate from the United Kingdom, was opposed to the convention because it required extraditing individuals for political offenses.[46] M. Hiorthoy, a delegate from Norway, stated, "The Norwegian delegation was of the opinion that the draft convention was too far-reaching."[47]

In other words, just as in 1972 a large majority of the United Nations did not consider terrorism to be a serious enough problem to be willing to take steps that could limit the freedom of action of countries vis-à-vis terrorist groups (i.e., the sort of steps that might prevent states from supporting terrorism), so too in 1937 the international community of nations was unwilling to abandon such traditional prerogatives as giving asylum to political offenders and allowing political exiles to circulate propaganda against their native land's regime. In both instances a consensus that terrorism was a problem of major proportions requiring prompt countermeasures did not exist.

Finally, it should be mentioned that there was one major difference between the way terrorism was debated in 1937 and the way it was debated in 1972: in 1937 there was an absence of concern about state-sponsored repression and terror.[48] Issues of terror by colonialist and racist regimes, which were extensively discussed in 1972, were ignored in 1937. The extent to which at the 1937 conference the issue of terrorism was divorced from the issue of colonialism is illustrated by the fact that Great Britain, the world's leading colonial power, opposed the convention. In contrast to the fears expressed by the coalition of Third World and communist states in 1972 that action against terrorism would benefit colonialist regimes, at the time of the 1937 Conference Great Britain apparently saw no connection between taking steps against terrorism and the defense of colonial empires.

The failure of the League of Nations convention would appear to indicate that there are enormous obstacles to effective multilateral measures against international terrorism: if in 1937, long before the current confrontation between the Third World and the industrialized world, there was no consensus that terrorism was a major problem, how much chance can there be of such a consensus developing today, given that terrorism is inextricably linked to the whole gamut of issues—imperialism, racism, and economic exploitation—over which this confrontation takes place? In other words, the evidence from the 1937 League of Nations convention indicates that the failure of American initiatives in the United Nations in the fall of 1972 was not due to any particular mistakes in the strategy or tactics of the way in which the American convention was introduced and defended but rather was due to a basic fact about the contemporary international system: not only is there presently no consensus among the community of nations that terrorism is a serious problem requiring effective countermeasures, but also it is most unlikely that there will be any such consensus in the foreseeable future.

NOTES

1. Interview No. 22 (Member of the American delegation to the United Nations).

2. See, for example, the American draft resolution on terrorism introduced in the United Nations in the fall of 1972, "United States of America:

Draft Resolution," General Assembly of the United Nations, 6th Committee, L.851, September 25, 1972.

3. John Dugard, "International Terrorism: Problems of Definition," *International Affairs*, Vol. 50, No. 1 (January 1974), p. 71; Carol Baumann, *The Diplomatic Kidnappings* (The Hague: Martinus Nijhoff, 1973), pp. 150-151.

4. *International and Transnational Terrorism: Diagnosis and Prognosis*, Central Intelligence Agency, 1976, p. 27.

5. Louis M. Bloomfield and Gerald F. Fitzgerald, *Crimes Against Internationally Protected Persons: Prevention and Punishment* (New York: Praeger Publishers, 1975), pp. 51-52.

6. *Department of State Bulletin*, June 1978, p. 60.

7. "American Draft Convention on Terrorism," *Department of State Bulletin*, October 16, 1972, p. 431 (Article 1).

8. Ibid., p. 431 (Article 1).

9. John R. Stevenson, "International Law and the Export of Terrorism," *Department of State Bulletin*, December 4, 1972, p. 651.

10. "American Draft Convention on Terrorism," p. 431 (Article 3).

11. Interview No. 22.

12. "United States of America: Draft Resolution."

13. William Rogers, "A World Free of Violence," *Department of State Bulletin*, October 16, 1972, p. 42.

14. *Official Records of the General Assembly*, 6th Committee, 27th Session, 1357 Meeting, pp. 254-255.

15. Ibid., 1362 Meeting, pp. 288-289.

16. Ibid., 1359 Meeting, p. 268.

17. Ibid., 1369 Meeting, p. 345.

18. Ibid., 1369 Meeting, p. 345.

19. Ibid., 1368 Meeting, pp. 335-336.

20. As a sidelight, mention might be made of the four nations that voted against the American initiatives yet did not mention the issue of wars of national liberation: Liberia, Malaysia, Nigeria, and Mexico. That these countries did not raise the question of wars of national liberation was hardly accidental; all of them have had or now have serious problems with revolutionary movements. Liberia's oligarchic political system has a number of domestic opponents, some of whom have ties to the more radical African states that are hostile to Liberia; Malaysia had a state of emergency during 1948-1960 due to a campaign by communist guerrillas; Nigeria had a bloody and prolonged civil war from 1967 to 1970; and Mexico has several urban and rural guerrilla groups.

21. *Official Records of the General Assembly*, 6th Committee, 27th Session, 1363 Meeting, p. 297.

22. Ibid., 1365 Meeting, p. 308.

23. Ibid., 1370 Meeting, p. 357.

24. Ibid., 1357 Meeting, p. 254.

25. Ibid.

26. Ibid., 1364 Meeting, pp. 300-301.

27. Ibid., 1366 Meeting, p. 323.

28. "Austria, Australia, Belgium, Canada, Costa Rica, Guatemala, Honduras, Iran, Italy, Japan, Luxemburg, New Zealand, Nicaragua and the United Kingdom of Great Britain and Northern Ireland: revised draft resolution," General Assembly of the United Nations, 6th Committee, L.879, Rev. 1, December 8, 1972.

29. Interview No. 22.

30. "Afghanistan, Algeria, Cameroon, Chad, Congo, Equatorial Guinea, Guinea, Guyana, India, Kenya, Madagascar, Mauritania, Mali, Sudan, Yugoslavia, Zambia: revised draft resolution," General Assembly of the United Nations, 6th Committee, L.880, Rev. 1, December 8, 1972.

31. Dugard, "International Terrorism," p. 74.

32. Interview No. 30 (Foreign Service Officer specializing in international legal affairs).

33. *Official Records of the General Assembly*, 6th Committee, 27th Session, passim.

34. Ibid.

35. Ibid., 1390 Meeting, p. 483, Vote on A, C.6, L.880, Rev. 1.

36. Ibid., 1389 Meeting, pp. 477-478.

37. Ibid. (emphasis added).

38. John R. Stevenson, "International Law and the Export of Terrorism," *Department of State Bulletin*, December 4, 1972, p. 645.

39. W. Tapley Bennett, Jr., "U.S. Initiatives in the United Nations to Combat International Terrorism," *International Lawyer*, Vol. 7, No. 4 (October 1973), p. 755.

40. For the text of the convention and the debates at the conference where it was adopted, see *Proceedings of the International Conference on the Repression of Terrorism* (Series of League of Nations Publications, C.94.M.47. Legal, V. 3, 1938).

41. Ibid., see pp. 71-83 for the debate on this article.

42. Ibid., p. 50.

43. Ibid., p. 60.

44. Ibid., p. 63.

45. Dugard, "International Terrorism," p. 69; Antoine Sottile, "Le Terrorisme International," *Academie de Droit International: Recueil des Cours,* Vol. 65, 1938 (III), pp. 137-138.

46. *Proceedings of the International Conference on the Repression of Terrorism,* p. 53.

47. Ibid., p. 88.

48. This absence was highly ironic, inasmuch as the League of Nations conference took place during the height of Stalin's Great Terror of 1936-1938.

chapter 8

TOWARD THE "REPOLITICAL-IZATION" OF AMERICAN POLICY RESPONSE TO INTERNATIONAL TERRORISM

If the United States wants to strengthen deterrence of acts of international terrorism, then it must first take into account the political factors behind the phenomenon of terrorism. Unless these factors are understood and acted upon, the pattern of failure in American policy response to transnational terrorism will continue.

In seeking to deter hostage incidents ("dual-phase" terrorist attacks), the United States must pursue a two-pronged strategy. The first prong of this strategy is to manipulate all of the rewards of such incidents, not simply the reward of prisoners and ransoms. The second prong must be to delegitimize hostage-taking as a strategy for revolutionary movements.

It was noted earlier that a frequent goal of terrorists in political kidnappings is to aggravate state-to-state relations in a given region. For example, Chapter 3 pointed out that the Palestinians who staged the Rome airport incident in December 1973 were apparently hoping to raise tensions in the Middle East so as to sabotage the upcoming Geneva peace conference. The proper way to deny terrorists this goal is for American policy makers to become more aware of the tactical objectives of a terrorist campaign. The large role played by the United States in world affairs makes it nationals a natural target for any terrorist group attempting to raise tensions in a region.

American policy makers must become aware of the fact that terrorists often will seek an American overreaction to an incident and must steel themselves to this fact and thereby deny the terrorists the desired overreaction.

The same "forewarned is forearmed" advice also applies to terrorist attacks designed to harass and intimidate the authorities of various nations. The United States should accept the fact that having Americans as military and civilian advisers to the security forces of other nations means that occasionally these advisers will be the target of attack by terrorist groups, and our leaders must not react to such attacks with alarm and surprise. To so react is to enable the terrorists to achieve their goal, inasmuch as the group that attacks the American advisers calculates that their attacks will shock U.S. policy makers to such an extent that they will be preoccupied with preventing another attack, hopefully to the point of withdrawing these advisers. In other words, American officials must not allow themselves to be so carried away by the passions that inevitably surround the killing by terrorists of Americans overseas that they lose sight of the long-range American foreign policy interests that led to the decision to station advisers in the country in question in the first place.

As for the terrorist objective of inciting governmental repression, the United States must do what it can to persuade foreign governments not to play into the hands of terrorists by instituting excessively repressive measures in response to terrorist incidents. As an example of American ability to convince other states to moderate repressive measures one might note the decision by Chile on November 17, 1976, to release 300 political prisoners. *The New York Times* pointed to American pressure on Chile, plus criticism from the United Nations and the Organization of American States, as "probable factors" influencing the decision of Chile to release the prisoners.[1]

There are major difficulties involved in any attempt to deny terrorists the publicity they seek by undertaking political kidnappings. If the terrorists desire *any* sort of publicity, then the chances of averting a violent resolution of a hostage situation are greatly reduced, because such a resolution inevitably produces much more publicity than a peaceful ending to a kidnapping, and hence the terrorists involved have less incentive to be accommodating. (The

fact that an ostensibly "unsuccessful" political kidnapping where
no concessions are made and the hostages are killed produces much
more publicity than a "successful" political kidnapping in which
the demands are met and the hostages released casts further discredit
upon American policy toward hostage incidents: the United States
has failed to recognize that if the terrorists receive enormous publicity from a kidnapping, then failing to get prisoners and/or ransoms does not mean that the kidnapping produced no benefits for
them.) However, in cases where the terrorists want *favorable*
publicity for their cause rather than just publicity, the United States
has a significant ability to manipulate the publicity reward of
political kidnappings. If the United States were to disavow its
policy of "no concessions" in favor of a more flexible policy of
making concessions in certain circumstances to terrorists holding
Americans hostage, this policy would strengthen deterrence of
political kidnappings by reducing the favorable publicity that
terrorist groups sometimes seek to attain by staging such kidnappings.

If the terrorists are to receive unfavorable publicity in hostage
situations, then it must be made clear to all that the risk of death to
which the hostages are exposed is solely the responsibility of the
terrorists. Very often terrorist groups try to put the blame on the
government in charge if there is a tragic outcome in a hostage situation by claiming that the government is responsible since it refused
to be reasonable. Consequently, a rigid, inflexible governmental
stance of "no concessions" plays right into the hands of the terrorists.
That governmental inflexibility often results in focusing the blame
of any possible tragedy on the government can be documented by
the following two cases: many Canadians blamed the rigidity and
the refusal to negotiate on the part of the Trudeau government for
the death of kidnapped Quebec minister Pierre LaPorte in the fall
of 1970,[2] and the *New York Times* was sharply critical of Kissinger's
intransigent stand during the incident involving the students who
were kidnapped in Tanzania and taken into Zaire.[3] In other words,
an American policy toward political kidnappings that was more
flexible than the current policy, that allowed concessions in some
instances to terrorists, would put the moral responsibility for any
deaths directly on the terrorists: they could not claim that the real
culprit was an inflexible and unreasonable government.

Such a policy does not mean giving in to any demands that a terrorist group may make. A policy of giving in on all demands would entail unacceptable costs. It would weaken deterrence of hostage situations; material rewards may be only one of five potential goals of a political kidnapping, but they are a very real goal nonetheless. Sometimes what is being demanded will simply be too great a price to pay for the safety of one or a few American nationals, for example, in the cases noted in Appendix II of the kidnapping of American citizens in Ethiopia and Thailand by secessionist movements, where the demand was for the United States to terminate military and economic assistance to the government of the nations where the kidnappings occurred. It will frequently be unwise to give in to demands because such a surrender would cause a serious rupture in the relations with the country where the hostage situation took place, for instance, the aggravation of relations between France and Chad over the kidnapping of Madame Claustre.

What this policy *does* mean is that the United States will not rule out in advance making any concessions to terrorists holding Americans hostage. Instead, American policy would be flexible: concessions would be made in certain instances if what was at stake was deemed to be especially important or if what was being asked was not significant. One case in which minor concessions settled a hostage incident without loss of life is the Hanafi Muslim incident in Washington, D.C., in March 1977. The Hanafis released their hostages after the authorities made three concessions: the Hanafi leader was paid $750 for earlier legal expenses, a film he considered sacreligious was stopped for one day, and he was allowed to return home after arraignment (he was carefully watched until properly jailed).[4] The alternative to these minor concessions was storming the three areas where the hostages were being held; the lives of many hostages could have been lost in such an operation. (Contrary to the myths that have grown up since the Entebbe raid, rescue operations are *always* high-risk propositions; for example, the death of nine Israeli athletes at the Munich airport and twenty-six Israeli children at Ma'alot.)

The second prong of an American policy to strengthen deterrence of hostage situations is to delegitimize hostage taking as a tactic for revolutionary groups. Proposals were discussed above to ensure that terrorists get bad publicity from political kidnappings. Delegitimizing hostage taking as a tactic goes beyond trying to manipulate the publicity on any given political kidnapping; instead, such a strategy of delegitimization will attempt to make the taking of hostages *always* appear to be wrong, regardless of whether the government involved was flexible or inflexible and regardless of who were the victims of the kidnappers.

ᶜThe strategy of delegitimizing hostage situations suggests itself from the history of the phenomenon of hijacking. When hijackings began on a large scale in the late 1960s there was initially much international sympathy for the hijackers. The Arab world claimed that the Palestinians had no other means to express their grievances against Israel. The Cubans claimed that those in the Americas who hijacked planes to Cuba were fleeing oppressive conditions in their own countries. Gradually, however, tolerance of hijacking declined. By the fall of 1978, ninety-five nations were party to The Hague anti-hijacking agreement and eighty-nine nations were party to the Montreal anti-aircraft sabotage agreement. In the early 1970s Cuba signed anti-hijacking accords with Colombia, Mexico, Venezuela, and the United States. The international consensus behind these various agreements is clear: hijackings are seen as an illegitimate means of attempting to rectify even serious and deeply felt political grievances.

In moving to delegitimize political kidnappings the United States should continue to support the efforts currently being made by the Federal Republic of Germany to draft an international convention against the taking of hostages. This proposal has been debated by a thirty-five member United Nations ad hoc committee since December 1976.[5] Should such a convention be agreed upon, it would be a powerful symbolic move toward delegitmizing the terrorist tactic of seizing hostages, in the same way that the various United Nations resolutions against hijacking and the three anti-hijacking conventions have served to do so.

However successful the above policy suggestions are in strengthening deterrence of hostage situations, they are irrelevant as a deterrence to "single-phase" terrorist acts in which there is no attempt to seize hostages. Since any attempt to get a multilateral convention against terrorism through the United Nations faces enormous obstacles, the question arises as to whether there is a method of deterring "single-phase" acts of terrorism besides multilateral conventions.

There is certainly one such alternative strategy, namely, the policy of reprisals carried out by the Israeli government against states that harbor and support Palestinian terrorists. Prior to Egyptian President Anwar Sadat's visit to Israel in November 1977 none of the Arab states were willing to accept Israel's right to exist; indeed, these states regarded themselves as being in a state of war with Israel. Given this lack of acceptance by her neighbors, Israel has felt that the only way to prevent Arab patronage of terrorist raids is to conduct reprisals against any Arab state that lends such patronage. Ze'ev Schiff, the military correspondent of the Israeli paper *Ha'aretz* and the author of some forty articles on Israel's reprisal policy, divides the history of the reprisal policy between 1949 and 1973 into five periods:[6]

A. 1949-1953: In this period there were a number of unorganized incursions into Israel by Palestinian refugees seeking revenge for having been forced into exile. The Israeli government, concerned lest morale suffer in the border settlements, sent raiding parties into Jordan and Lebanon to attack the villages from which the raiders came and thereby to give warning to those living in these villages not to tolerate future raids. During this period the Israelis did not publicly admit that they were undertaking reprisal actions.

B. 1953-1954: This was a transition period in which the reprisal policy gave rise to a special "101" unit to carry out reprisals. Moshe Dayan, at this time the chief of staff, laid down the doctrinal rationale for reprisals:

1. The Arabs only understood force.
2. Restraint on the part of Israel will be seen as a sign of weakness and fear and will encourage further attacks.
3. For reprisals to be effective several Arabs must be killed for each dead Israeli

C. 1954-1956: This period began in the aftermath of a raid against the town of Qibya in Jordan in 1954. This particular reprisal caused a great deal of discussion in Israel because a number of civilians were killed. The reprisals in 1954-1956 were directed away from civilian targets and toward military targets. The reprisals were now explicitly aimed at the Arab governments and not, as before, against the populations of the villages from which the raiders came. Dayan stated that the purpose of the reprisals was to make Arab governments pay a high price for shedding Israeli blood.

D. 1956-1967: After the 1956 war, Israel's borders were quiet for some eight years; however, with the beginning of al Fatah's raids in early 1965, reprisals began again. The 1966 reprisal against the town of Samu in Jordan was a major contributing cause to the 1967 war.

E. 1967-1973: In this period between the Six Day and the Yom Kippur wars the Israeli policy toward *fedayeen* raids moved beyond the concept of reprisals and began to approach that of full-scale warfare. Airplanes and artillery were used to attack *fedayeen* bases in Lebanon and Jordan. The Israelis assassinated Palestinian leaders in Beirut and elsewhere.

Dan Horowitz of the Hebrew University of Jerusalem and Barry Blechman of the Arms Control and Disarmament Agency have both concluded that the Israeli reprisal policy has in several instances resulted in a lessening of terrorist incidents. In an interview with Horowitz he stated that his research indicated that the reprisals against Jordan in the period 1949-1956 were effective in reducing the incident of *fedayeen* infiltration from Jordan into Israel.[7] Blechman's unpublished Ph.D. dissertation on Israeli reprisal policy argued that Israeli reprisals between 1950 and 1954 and between 1965 and 1967 were successful in getting the bordering Arab states to take steps to curb infiltration into Israel by Palestinian terrorists.[8] Blechman went on to argue, however, that the reprisals' impact on the behavior of the Arab nations was usually limited in duration— that "in most cases" the effect of the reprisals on the target nation's behavior was dissipated after 30 days.[9]

This evidence from Israeli experiences indicates that a policy of unilateral reprisals and retaliatory raids can have a deterrent effect against terrorist attacks. In terms of the deterrence formula $C + R > B$, the reprisals have the effect of raising the $C + R$ side of the formula for the countries giving sanctuary and support to the terrorists and thereby reducing the willingness of such countries to back terrorist actions against other countries. But a policy of reprisals also has two major costs which together make such a policy very unattractive for the United States. The first cost is that the reprisals can escalate international tensions to such a degree that war may result. The Israeli reprisals in 1955-1956 and in 1965-1967, for example, were a major factor in the escalation process that led to the 1956 and 1967 Middle East wars. Given the demonstrated fact that reprisals can raise tensions to the point of war, the United States would be undertaking grave risks if it were to adopt a reprisal policy in response to terrorist incidents against its nationals.

A second major cost of a policy of reprisals is that such a policy aggravates the relations of the state undertaking the reprisal with normally friendly states. Such an aggravation of relations has clearly been the case with Israel and its policy of reprisals. Not only do these reprisals invariably result in sharp criticsm of Israel in the United Nations,[10] but also on two occasions reprisals have broken off a relationship between Israel and an arms supplier. In October 1955 Foreign Minister Sharett of Israel flew to Geneva where the Big Four (Britain, France, the United States, and the Soviet Union) were meeting. Israel, seriously alarmed by the Czech arms deal with Egypt, was seeking arms from the Western powers. At first the United States seemed favorably disposed toward providing Israel with arms. In December 1955 Sharett went to Washington for further discussions on an arms sale. On December 17, 1955, Israel staged a reprisal near Lake Tiberias. "Diplomatic opinion agreed at the time that the reprisal had sabotaged the possibility of a U.S.-Israel [arms] arrangement."[11] In the aftermath of the Beirut airport reprisal in December 1968, the French government placed a total embargo on the shipment of arms and spare parts to Israel.[12] In interviews in October 1975 Israeli officials agreed that it was true that Israeli reprisals caused problems with other countries, but they argued that domestic considerations were sufficiently important to outweigh the international condemnation of these reprisals. They noted the need to maintain morale in the face of the terrorist campaign by striking back at the terrorists and those who supported them and the need to protect the population.[13] One official quoted Golda Meir's statement, "I would rather have my children alive than care about world public opinion."[14]

Reprisals aggravate relations between the nation undertaking the reprisal and usually friendly states because the current international system accords little legitimacy to the right of reprisal, although there is still a debate among international lawyers over the legality of reprisals. However, in his review of this debate Blechman concluded that the majority of contemporary legal scholars believe that the United Nations Charter outlaws resort to reprisals.[15]

The lack of legitimacy accorded to reprisals and retaliatory raids means that a nation resorting to such actions runs the risk of being branded as an international outlaw. As a small and highly unpopular nation, Israel feels that it does not have a great deal to lose by undertaking reprisals, and so it continues to do so. However, the United States, dependent as it is on good relations with a number of countries around the world to protect its economic, military, and political interests, could not afford the sort of massive international criticisms and condemnation that would certainly greet any American policy of systematically undertaking reprisals for terrorist incidents. The domestic furor that such a policy would generate also would impede the conduct of American foreign policy.

In light of the unacceptably high costs of attempting to achieve deterrence of terrorist incidents by unilateral reprisals and raids, the United States has no alternative but to go on trying to negotiate multilateral accords against terrorism. However, if the United States wants effective multilateral action against terrorism, it must be prepared to conduct negotiations in a political sense rather than in a humanitarian sense. That is, it must abandon the assumption that all nations see terrorism as a serious problem requiring prompt countermeasures and instead start from the assumption that if there is to be effective multilateral action against terrorism, then the United States must be prepared to use the same sort of standard "carrot and stick" inducements in negotiations on terrorism that are used in other types of negotiations. If the United States were to carry on its negotiations in such a political sense, then there would be three possible areas in which multilateral action could be taken against terrorism: (a) bilateral accords, (b) action by the Western nations to put teeth into existing accords, and (c) regional accords.

A bilateral accord that illustrates the difference between treating terrorism as if it were a humanitarian issue and treating it as if it were a political issue is the Cuban-American anti-hijacking accord that was signed on February 15, 1973. In the negotiations on this accord there was no automatic assumption by U.S. officials that there existed a consensus between the United States and Cuba over the need to stop hijackings. Instead, American negotiators realized that if there was to be an accord there must be a process of mutual political concessions. So in return for Castro's agreement to extradite or prosecute hijackers the United States agreed to crack down on the various groups of Cuban exiles who were organizing raids against Cuban targets.[16] (On October 6, 1976, a Cuban airliner was blown up while in flight, killing everyone on board. Castro was convinced that the plane had been sabotaged by Cuban exiles and was angered at what he regarded as an American failure to honor its commitment to crack down on the terrorist activities of Cuban exiles. Consequently, he abrogated the U.S.-Cuban anti-hijacking accord on October 15, 1976. However, he announced that Cuba would continue to refuse to grant sanctuary to hijackers.)[17]

The Cuban-American accord on hijacking is instructive for several reasons. It shows that if the United States is willing to offer substantive concessions on other issues, then joint action against terrorism is possible even with nations that enjoy very poor relations with the United States. Cuban-American relations have been so poor that the negotiations on the hijacking agreement were conducted through third parties. It indicates that even nations like Cuba that are highly sympathetic to revolutionary movements will not necessarily put the cause of world revolution ahead of their state interests. And there are two groups of evidence which indicate that an international convention such as the Cuban-American anti-hijacking accord can be an effective deterrent to terrorist actions. The first set of evidence is that after the signing of the Cuban-American accord on February 15, 1973, the number of hijackings from the United States to Cuba went down sharply,[18] as Table VIII shows. However, given that most of the hijackings from the United States to Cuba were by psychotics or criminals, the evidence from this table is not conclusive when it comes to the effectiveness of international conventions as a deterrent to acts of terrorism.

A significantly more conclusive set of evidence is supplied by analyzing the impact of accords signed between Cuba and three other Latin American states. Cuba signed hijacking accords with Mexico on June 7, 1973,[19] with Venezuela on July 6, 1973,[20] and with Colombia on July 22, 1974.[21] In order to evaluate the effec-

American Policy Response

TABLE VIII.   *Incidence of Attempted Hijackings from the*
              United States to Cuba, 1968-1974

1968	1969	1970	1971	1972	1973	1974
23	37	14	29	29	2	7

Source: *Strategic Survey* (London: International Institute for Strategic Studies, 1975), p. 90.

tiveness of these accords the *New York Times* index was reviewed for a certain period before and after each accord to check for instances of politically motivated hijackings to Cuba. In the case of the Cuban-Mexican accord, the period December 7, 1969, to June 6, 1973, was scanned to note instances of hijackings before the accord; the period June 7, 1973, to December 6, 1976, was reviewed for instances after the accord. Each period came to a total of 42 months. For the Cuban-Venezuelan accord, the periods scrutinized were January 6, 1970, to July 5, 1973, and July 6, 1973, to January 5, 1977, with 42 months before and 42 months after; while for the Cuban-Colombian accord, the periods scanned were July 22, 1972, to July 21, 1974, and July 22, 1974, to July 21, 1976, with 24 months before and 24 months after. The total amount of time examined for the three bilateral accords was 108 months before their signing and 108 months after. In the periods of time before these accords there were nine politically motivated hijackings between Cuba and one of these three countries, while in the time periods after the accords there were none.

Another avenue of possible multilateral action against terrorism is for the leading Western nations to cooperate to put sanctions against nations that support terrorism. These nations are in agreement about the need to take steps against terrorism, and hence action by them can take place without the logjams over wars of national liberation that have plagued United Nations efforts on terrorism.

A promising example of such Western cooperation is the agreement on hijacking reached at the Bonn summit of the major industrialized powers in July 1978. The nations represented at the summit (the United States, Canada, Japan, Great Britain, Italy, West Germany, and France) agreed to cut off air service by their airlines to nations that refuse to extradite or punish hijackers. They also pledged to stop all flights by any other airliners between their own countries and such sanctuary states. Given that these seven nations account for approximately 75 percent of the world's commercial air traffic, such a sanction would represent a significant loss to a country.[22]

Finally, the United States should encourage regional pacts in Western Europe and in Latin America against terrorism. There is already a consensus among most of the nations of Western Europe and Latin America that steps must be taken against terrorism. For example, in the vote in the Sixth Committee of the United Nations on terrorism in the fall of 1972 all of the Western European nations either voted in favor of prompt action against international terrorism or abstained. A majority of the Latin American and Carribean states did likewise.[23] (Several of the states in the Americas that voted against such prompt action in 1972 have since been supportive of measures against terrorism.)[24]

Given this existing consensus in Western Europe and in the Americas in favor of steps against terrorism, the United States should seek further ratifications to existing regional accords and should try to strengthen these accords. In the Americas the United States should encourage more countries to ratify the Organization of American States Convention to Prevent and Punish Acts of Terrorism Taking the Form of Crimes Against Persons and Related Extortion that Are of International Significance. This treaty, which was signed in 1971 and entered into force in 1973, has been ratified by only six states. In addition to urging more states to ratify this convention, the United States should seek to strengthen it by expanding its scope beyond the protection of diplomats to encompass acts of international terrorism in general.[25] In Western Europe the United States should urge more states to ratify the Council of Europe's Convention on the Suppression of Terrorism. This convention, which currently has three ratifications, was adopted by the Council of Europe in 1976 and came into effect in 1977. The

United States also should seek to reduce the number of exceptions allowed in the extradition clauses of this convention.[26]

Effective regional pacts in the Americas and in Western Europe would be a crippling blow against international terrorism, inasmuch as a heavily disproportionate amount of the international terrorism of the past decade has taken place in Latin America and Western Europe. A CIA study on terrorism that was released in August 1978 estimated that 64 percent of the international terrorist incidents in the period 1968-1977 took place in Western Europe or in Latin America.[27]

NOTES

1. *New York Times*, November 18, 1976.
2. John Saywell, *Quebec 70* (Toronto: University of Toronto Press, 1970), p. 136.
3. *New York Times*, August 14, 1975.
4. Brooks McClure, "Terrorism Today and Tomorrow: Prognosis and Treatment," in *Contemporary Terrorism*, ed. John Elliott and Leslie Gibson (Gaithersburg, Maryland; International Association of Chiefs of Police, 1978), p. 296.
5. Interview No. 30 (Foreign Service Officer specializing in International legal affairs).
6. Interview No. 42 (Ze'ev Schiff).
7. Interview No. 37 (Dan Horowitz).
8. Barry Blechman, *The Consequences of Israeli Reprisals: An Assessment* (Ph.D. dissertation, Georgetown University, 1971), p. 144.
9. Ibid., pp. 178-179.
10. Ibid., pp. 197-198.
11. Ibid., pp. 215-216.
12. Ibid., p. 214.
13. Interviews No. 38, 39, and 40 (Officials in the Israeli Ministry of Foreign Affairs).
14. Interview No. 40.
15. Blechman, *Israeli Reprisals*, p. 59.
16. For the text of the hijacking pact, see "Hijacking Accord Between the United States and Cuba," hearings before the Subcommittee on Inter-

American Affairs of the Committee on Foreign Affairs, House of Representatives, 93rd Congress, February 20, 1973.

17. Interview No. 30.

18. The hijacker profile also came into use in early 1973, and some
authorities have argued that it—rather than the Cuban-American accord—
cut down the number of hijackings. However, David Hubbard, the creator
of the hijacker profile, stated in a presentation at the CUNY conference
on terrorism in June 1976 that the major factor in reducing hijackings to
Cuba was the anti-hijacking accord.

19. *Facts on File*, Vol. 33, No. 1701 (1973), p. 523.

20. Ibid., Vol. 33, No. 1705 (1973), p. 652.

21. Ibid. Vol. 34, No. 1762 (1974), p. 674.

22. Interview No. 30.

23. *Official Records of the General Assembly*, 6th Committee, 27th
Session, 1390 Meeting, p. 483. Vote on A, C.6, L.880, Rev. 1.

24. Interview No. 30.

25. *International and Transnational Terrorism: Diagnosis and Prognosis*, Central Intelligence Agency, April 1976, p. 27.

26. *International Terrorism in 1977*, Central Intelligence Agency, August
1978, p. 5.

27. Ibid., p. 2.

chapter 9

CONCLUSION

As J. Bowyer Bell has pointed out, revolutionary leaders and movements are surrounded by a great deal of mythology. The policy response of the United States to international terrorism has been determined by two such myths about the phenomenon of terrorism: that most terrorist incidents are the product of either criminal or psychotic antisocial individuals and that terrorism is perceived as a humanitarian problem by the great majority of the nations of the world. These American myths about terrorism have led to efforts to deter acts of terrorism by "depoliticized" methods. An attempt was made to deter kidnappings ("dual-phase" terrorist acts) by denying terrorist the rewards that supposedly were the objective of such kidnappings, and efforts were made to deter terrorist incidents that did not involve the taking of hostages ("single-phase" terrorist acts) by supporting multilateral conventions that treat terrorist incidents as ordinary crimes.

The central thrust of this book has been that American efforts to deter acts of international terrorism have been largely unsuccessful because they have been based on the assumption that terrorism is not a political phenomenon. Terrorism, this book has argued, is a rational strategy of achieving political goals through violence and is so regarded by the great majority of the nations of the world.

The question arises as to why American policy toward international terrorism has been founded on such unsound assumptions. The answer to this question lies in the historical experience of the United States. In the late 1960s the slogan "violence is as American as cherry pie" was widely proclaimed both as an explanation of and as a justification for the racial and student violence of those years. This slogan is a misleading half-truth. Specifically, it ignores two of the most salient facts about violence in America. First, most American violence has been pro status quo and, second, there are few or no instances in American history of groups resorting to any of the four strategies of violent social change outlined in the introduction to this book.

The pro status quo violence in America has taken a number of forms:

A. There has been a large amount of what can be called "nativist" violence, that is, violence by the economically and socially dominant white Protestant ethnic group against newly arriving immigrant groups. In 1834 a mob in Boston sacked and burned the Ursuline Catholic Convent. In 1891 a group of eleven Italian immigrants were lynched in New Orleans. In 1943 there were several days of rioting directed against Mexicans by white citizens in Los Angeles.[1]

B. The history of the labor movement in America frequently has been marked by violence against unions. In the Pullman strike of 1894 federal troops and state milita were used to break the strike; in the course of the strike some thirty-four people died. In the Ludlow strike in the Colorado coal fields in 1913-1914 a total of seventy-four individuals were killed in clashes between strikers and the private armies of the coal field operators. On Memorial Day in 1937 the Chicago police killed ten strikers outside the Republic steel plant on the South Side.[2]

C. Violence against blacks by whites who feared changes in race relations has been a common occurrence in American history. In the Reconstruction period thousands of blacks were killed by supporters of white supremacy. In Wilmington, North Carolina, in 1898, following the appointment of a number of blacks to local political offices, mobs of whites killed dozens of blacks and forced all local black office holders to resign. The East St. Louis race riot of 1917, sparked by the fears of whites that blacks immigrating from the south were taking their jobs away, left some forty-eight people dead.[3]

D. Movements seeking major changes in American society have often been the target of violence by those opposed to change. In New York in 1834 mobs destroyed the homes and businesses of a number of abolitionists. On May Day in 1919 a number of parades by Socialist party members were attacked by crowds angry over the socialists' refusal to support American involvement in World War I. The years after World War I also witnessed frequent incidents of violence against the radical unionists of the Industrial Workers of the World.[4]

In reply to the above argument that most American violence has been pro status quo it could be claimed that there are two major exceptions to this generalization, namely, the American Revolution and the Civil War. However, even these two wars were oriented far more toward protecting the status quo than toward instituting a new social order. The American Revolution was sparked by British attempts to reduce and restrict the long-established rights of the colonies. In this respect the American colonies were really fighting to retain what they already had, a fact recognized by British conservative Edmund Burke in his defense of the struggle of the colonies against George III and his government. Similarly, the eleven states of the Confederacy seceded from the Union when they feared that the new presidency of Abraham Lincoln and the Republicans would attempt to abolish the existing right of citizens in the slave states to own slaves.

The introduction to this book outlined four strategies of violent social and political change: the coup d'etat, the insurrection, guerrilla warfare, and terrorism. A striking fact about American history is that there are few or no instances of groups out of power attempting to achieve their arms by resorting to one of these strategies. There has never been a military coup d'etat in the United States. The United States has experienced the insurrections of the American colonies and of the South, but two facts are noteworthy about these insurrections: first, as was noted above, these insurrections were in defense of established rights rather than an attempt to establish a new social and political order; and second, these revolts were caused by the desire of one part of a political system (the American colonies and the South) to break away from the central authorities of the system (the British monarchy and the federal government in Washington) rather than by a desire to overthrow these central authorities. In these respects the American Revolution and the Civil War were very different from the French Revolution of 1789 and the Russian Revolution of 1917. The latter revolutions had the radical social goal of overthrowing the government of the political system and creating a new economic and political order, while the former revolts had the conservative social goal of breaking away from the existing political system so as to preserve the established economic and political order.

As for guerrilla warfare and terrorism, here again there are few instances of such violence in the history of American society. The two major wars fought on American soil, the American Revolution and the Civil War, were conducted almost entirely by conventional military forces and strategies; guerrilla operations were peripheral in both conflicts. Unlike Spain during the Napoleonic wars or South Africa during the Boer War, where the defeat of these nations' regular armies was followed by a prolonged period of guerrilla war, when the South's regular armies surrendered the Civil War came to an end. And while there have been groups in American history that have engaged in terrorism (such as the Ku Klux Klan and the Molly Maguires), in the main such groups have acted out of local concerns rather than out of a desire to bring down the central government. As Walter Laqueur has stated: ". . . terrorism in the United States was limited in scope and purpose; there was no intention of overthrowing the government, killing the political leadership or changing the political system."[5]

Given the lack of any significant historical experience with political violence undertaken to effect revolutionary changes in society, the reaction of American officials to the resurgence of international terrorism in the late 1960s apparently was to relate the phenomenon of terrorism to the types of violence that were common in American society in the 1960s and 1970s: criminal violence, psychotic violence, and violence stemming from unfocused social resentment and anger. In the late 1960s large yearly increases in violent crime began to take place in the United States. Violence by psychotics in the form of airplane hijackings and ritualistic murders by individuals such as Charles Manson and his followers was common and was given widespread coverage in the media. And in the late 1960s there were serious race riots in Watts, Detroit, Newark, and other cities and major student disturbances at Berkeley, Columbia, Cornell, Harvard, and other colleges. This racial and student unrest was clearly grounded in political concerns, but it was not aimed at achieving a given list of goals or based on a specific group of grievances; instead this unrest reflected a rather vague and unstructured resentment over the way American society operated.

In light of the sort of violence that characterized American society in the 1960s and 1970s the reaction of American policy makers to the wave of incidents of international terrorism that began in the late 1960s becomes understandable. Earlier it was noted that American officials frequently have referred to terrorist acts as "ordinary crimes." Such acts also frequently have been called "senseless": in official statements issued after the deaths of the U.S. ambassador to Lebanon and two members of the embassy staff in June 1976, after the assassination by Palestinian terrorists of four people including an American citizen at the Istanbul airport in August 1976, and after the killings of a number of Israelis on a bus in Israel in March 1978, the word "senseless" was used to describe the killings.[6] This rhetoric describing terrorist acts as "criminal" and "senseless" is rooted in the historical experiences of the United States: the violence in America in the 1960s and 1970s, like most of the violence in American history, was not in any sense purposive violence designed to achieve certain changes in the existing social and political order. Instead, this violence of recent decades had its origins in criminal behavior, mental illness, and a generalized and amorphous bitterness toward society.

If the United States is to achieve a more effective structure of deterrence against international terrorism, then it must begin by realizing that its own national experience has been a poor guide to the problem of terrorism. The United States must reject the "depoliticized" approach to terrorism that stems from the application of an inappropriate national historical experience and must instead face up to the complex set of political factors behind the phenomenon of international terrorism.

NOTES

1. Richard Hofstadter and Michael Wallace, *American Violence* (New York: Vintage Books, 1971), pp. 298-301 and 332-338.

2. Ibid., pp. 151-156, 160-164, and 179-184.

3. Ibid., pp. 223-224, 230-236, and 241-245.

4. Ibid., pp. 341-344 and 351-356.

5. Walter Laqueur, *Terrorism* (Boston: Little Brown & Company, 1977), p. 15.

6. "Statement by President Ford," *Department of State Bulletin*, July 19, 1976, p. 98; "U.S. Condemns Terrorist Attack at Istanbul Airport," *Department of State Bulletin*, August 30, 1976, p. 293; "Letter (by President Carter) to Prime Minister Begin," *Department of State Bulletin*, May 1978, p. 46.

appendix I

BIBLIOGRAPHIC ESSAY

Anyone doing research on a topic as surrounded by controversy as terrorism must take particular care with his or her sources. To attempt to argue from one set of materials is virtually certain to lead to serious distortions of the topic. In an effort to avoid such distortions, this book has drawn from the following seven groups of data:

A. Interviews with revolutionaries and with government officials. In the course of two trips overseas, the first to Israel and the second to Ireland, I interviewed a number of both currently active and retired revolutionary leaders. In Ireland the individuals interviewed were mostly members of the various branches of the Republican movement, but several Protestant paramilitaries also were contacted. In Israel two former members of the Zionist Underground were interviewed.

A number of government officials from the United States, Israel, and Great Britain were consulted. The officials interviewed had all had some sort of direct involvement with the problem of terrorism as it affected their respective countries.

Several of those interviewed requested anonymity, and so their names were not placed after the interview number. Appendix IV gives a brief description of all of the individuals interviewed for this book.

B. Official government documents. The central concern of this book has been the reaction of the American government to international terrorism, and consequently it was imperative to examine official documents, both for the information they themselves could provide and as a check on the information gathered in interviews. Three major groups of official documents were examined. The first was the statements and press releases put out by various American officials in response to major terrorist incidents. (The source used for these statements and press releases was the *Department of State Bulletin.*) The second group of documents was speeches by American and other delegations in the Sixth Committee of the United Nations during the debate on terrorism in the fall of 1972. These Sixth Committee speeches are perhaps the best available documentation of the enormous difficulties involved in reaching any sort of consensus among the nations of the world about action against terrorism.

A third set of official documents that was found to be very useful was the report issued by the League of Nations concerning its conference on terrorism in 1937. (See *Proceedings of the International Conference on the Repression of Terrorism,* Series of League of Nations Publications, C.94, M.47, Legal, V.3, 1938.) This conference report is very valuable as a corrective to the contemporary tendency to regard terrorism as a wholly new phenomenon. Reading the speeches and comments in this report reveals that many of the concerns about and interpretations of terrorism that are widespread today also were current in 1937.

C. Documents by revolutionary groups. Revolutionaries have one thing in common with academics: both are haunted by a "publish or perish" syndrome. For a revolutionary movement to survive, grow, and achieve its goals it must make a continuous effort to explain and justify its cause. Hence the unceasing stream of interviews, manifestos, and articles flowing from underground groups. This book has sought to tap this stream by reading the releases and manifestos published at the time of various terrorist incidents by the groups responsible for the incidents. (The basic source for such releases and manifestos was the Foreign Broadcast Information Service's daily reports on various regions of the world.)

There is a small group of documents by prominent revolutionaries that is of sufficient importance to be commented upon individually. Frantz Fanon's *The Wretched of the Earth* (New York: Grove Press, 1966), is perhaps the single most important revolutionary manifesto of the post-World War II period. Fanon's vivid prose provides an ideological justification for revolutionary violence. Ernesto Ché Guevara's *Guerrilla Warfare* (New York: Vintage Press, 1961), does not have much in it that is original, but the book is important because it has been widely used (and misused) by revolutionaries during the 1960s and 1970s. And Carlos Marighella's "Minimanual of the Urban Guerrilla" (London: International Institute for Strategic Studies, 1971) has been a handbook for strategy and tactics for contemporary urban guerrilla groups. Anyone who desires to "read up" on terrorism would do well to begin with these works by Fanon, Guevara, and Marighella.

D. Memoirs. Provided one reads them with discretion because of their inevitably self-justificatory nature, memoirs can provide a valuable source of data. Menachem Begin's *The Revolt: The Story of the Irgun* (Jerusalem: Steimatzky's Agency Limited, 1972) gives Begin's side of the struggle of the Zionist Underground. Given the controversy surrounding many of the events these memoirs describe, they should be read in conjunction with other accounts of the same period. A particularly good recent account of the Zionist Underground is J. Bowyer Bell's *Terror Out of Zion* (New York: St. Martin's Press, 1977). Whatever bias they may have, Begin's memoirs are important because they have been read by revolutionary groups as diverse as the IRA and the Tupamaros. George Grivas' *Memoirs of General Grivas* (New York: Frederick A. Praeger, 1965) are interesting and insightful, but like Begin's memoirs the events they describe are very controversial and hence they too should be read in conjunction with other accounts of these events. See, for example, the chapter on Cyprus in J. Bowyer Bell's *On Revolt* (Cambridge, Massachusetts: Harvard University Press, 1976).

Ché Guevara's *The Diary of Ché Guevara* (New York: Ramparts Magazine, 1968) does not provide much in the way of insight into or comment upon the major strategical and tactical concerns of revolutionary leaders. This lack of insight is undoubtedly due to the very trying conditions of the Bolivian campaign during which the diary was written. The chief value of the diary is that reading it should—due to its account of the dreary, tiring, and at times desperate life of a guerrilla fighter—dispel once and for all the romantic "myth of the guerrilla."

Leila Khaled's *My People Shall Live* (London: Hodden and Staughton, 1973) does not add much new information concerning the Arab-Israeli dispute or the Palestinian movement. The book's redeeming characteristic is that it has a great deal of revealing data about Khaled herself; and given that she is one of the most interesting revolutionary fighters of recent years, that fact makes the book worthwhile. Sean MacStiofain's *Revolutionary in Ireland* (Edinburgh, Scotland: R & R Clark, Ltd., 1975) is valuable on two counts: first, it gives MacStiofain's interpretations of the development of the Ulster problem during the years 1970 to 1972 in which he was chief of staff of the Provisional IRA and, second, it tells one a great deal about the background of MacStiofain who, like Leila Khaled, is one of the most significant revolutionaries of the past decade.

The previously mentioned memoirs are by individuals who engaged in revolutionary struggles. The last book of memoirs to be noted, Geoffrey Jackson's *Surviving the Long Night* (New York: Vanguard Press, 1974), is by an individual who was the victim of a revolutionary struggle. Jackson's

account of his eight-month captivity at the hands of the Tupamaro guerrillas contains some interesting information about the Tupamaros, but the
real value of the book is its insight into the relations between captive and
captor during a political kidnapping.

E. Literature on political violence and on international affairs. The literature on problems of political violence is so vast that it is hard to know
where to begin. One good place to start reading is with Ted Robert Gurr's
Why Men Rebel (Princeton: Princeton University Press, 1970) and with
Samuel P. Huntington's *Political Order in Changing Societies* (New Haven:
Yale University Press, 1968). The merit of both books is that they provide
an innovative theoretical framework on questions of political violence and
then support this framework with a vast wealth of historical data and social
science research.

Walter Z. Laqueur has put together a four-volume study on guerrilla
warfare and terrorism. He wrote two of the volumes, *Terrorism* (Boston:
Little, Brown and Company, 1977) and *Guerrilla* (Boston: Little, Brown
and Company, 1976), and he edited two others, *The Terrorism Reader*
(New York: Meridian Books, 1978) and *The Guerrilla Reader* (New York:
Meridian Books, 1977). These four books provide a very useful and insightful discussion of guerrilla war and terrorism. They are well written and are
particularly valuable because Laqueur discusses the contemporary resurgence of terrorism with reference to earlier historical instances of this form
of violence.

The single most valuable work on deterrence literature for this book was
by Alexander L. George and Richard Smoke, *Deterrence in American
Foreign Policy: Theory and Practice* (New York: Columbia University
Press, 1974). The major accomplishment of George and Smoke was to lift
writing on deterrence out of the ruts that were established in the early
1960s. The book breaks a lot of new ground, particularly in its disucssions
of rationality and deterrence and in its analysis of the post-World War II
deterrence literature.

Chapter 4 on terrorism and international politics drew on several bodies
of international relations literature. The accounts of the escalatory poten-
tial of terroristic violence in the Middle East are in large part drawn from
the following works on Middle Eastern politics: Barry Blechman, *The
Consequences of Israeli Reprisals: An Assessment* (Ph.D. dissertation,
Georgetown University, 1971); Yair Evron, *The Middle East: Nations,
Superpowers, and Wars* (New York: Praeger Publishers, 1973); and
Walter Z. Laqueur, *The Road to Jerusalem* (New York: The Macmillan
Company, 1968). Blechman's dissertation is a systematic evaluation of
Israel's reprisal policy, and hence it is indispensable reading for anyone

who seeks to evaluate the role that the Palestinians have played in the Arab-Israeli conflict. The works by Laqueur and Evron are valuable because they both provide reasonably detached and objective accounts of some of the major events of the Arab-Israeli dispute.

Chapter 4 also discussed the idea of "surrogate warfare." The phrase itself and the concept behind the phrase are drawn from Brian Jenkins' *International Terrorism: A New Mode of Conflict* (Los Angeles: Crescent Publications, 1975). In addition to the surrogate warfare concept, this pamphlet contains a number of interesting insights that make it well worth reading.

F. Chronologies of terrorist incidents. This book has made use of three chronologies of terrorist incidents. The first is Brian Jenkins and Janera Johnson's *International Terrorism: A Chronology, 1968-1974* (Santa Monica, California: The RAND Corporation, 1975). Second, the office of the special assistant to the Secretary of State for combatting terrorism has put together two chronologies of terrorist incidents involving American nationals. (See *Chronology of Attacks Upon Non-Official American Citizens* and *Chronology of Significant Terrorist Incidents Involving U.S. Diplomatic/Official Personnel.* These two State Department chronologies are in unpublished manuscript form.) Finally, this book has used a chronology of international terrorist incidents put together by Edward Mickolus of Yale University as part of his doctoral dissertation.

G. Secondary source accounts of various revolutionary movements. As a hedge against being led astray by interviews with revolutionaries and by the propaganda tracts of revolutionary movements, it is advisable for anyone researching these movements to read secondary source accounts. One very good such account about an important contemporary revolutionary movement is J. Bowyer Bell's *The Secret Army: The IRA, 1916-1974* (Cambridge, Massachusetts: The M.I.T. Press, 1974). Bell had the good fortune of getting in "on the ground floor" with the IRA, that is, he started his research on the Republican movement before the current "troubles" began in Ireland. Consequently, his sources and contacts in the IRA's two branches are excellent. The book itself is well written and very informative.

A useful study of the Palestinian movement is *The Politics of Palestinian Nationalism* by William B. Quandt, Fuad Jabber, and Ann Mosely Lesch (Berkeley: University of California Press, 1972). The authors realize that an understanding of past history is essential to comprehending the present acts of a revolutionary organization. Hence they have several chapters on the development of Palestinian national consciousness and activism in the period from the Balfour Declaration until the emergence of the contemporary *fedayeen* movement. The only real problem with Quandt et al. is that their book was published in 1972 and hence only carries the history of the Palestinian movement up until 1970-1971; one hopes that there will be an updated edition.

A final secondary source account that is quite worthwhile is Arturo C. Porzecanski's *Uruguay's Tupamaros* (New York: Praeger Publishing Company, 1973). Porzecanski's discussion of the rise and fall of the Tupamaros is fair and balanced. Perhaps the most valuable part of the book is a series of tables detailing the age, sex, class status, and occupational experience of the Tupamaros. These tables are valuable because they are a nugget of hard data in a vast stream of speculation as to the background of contemporary urban terrorists.

In sum, the multiplicity of sources, all of which served as cross-checks on each other, provided enough worthwhile data to do serious academic work on American policy toward international terrorism, despite the controversy with which the topic is surrounded.

appendix II
SUMMARY OF THE INCIDENTS OF TERRORISM INVOLVING WEST GERMANS, JAPANESE, AND AMERICANS RECORDED IN TABLE IV IN CHAPTER 6

This appendix summarizes the hostage-taking incidents that were used to make up Table IV in Chapter 6. Table IV recorded the number of governmental and private hostage situations involving the Federal Republic of Germany between April 1, 1970, and March 31, 1975. There were, in all, ten incidents of hostage taking that involved direct or indirect demands on the West German government and two incidents that involved demands on private parties.

The cases in which direct or indirect concessions were demanded from the West German government are as follows:

1. West German Ambassador to Brazil Ehrenfried von Hollenben was kidnapped by Brazilian terrorists on June 11, 1970. He was released after the Brazilian government flew forty prisoners to Algeria.

2. Bolivian terrorists kidnapped two West German technicians in Teoponte on July 21, 1970. The technicians were released after the Bolivian government freed ten prisoners.

3. One of the PFLP's demands in the four hijackings of September 1970 was for West Germany to free three Palestinian terrorists captured by the Federal Republic's authorities in an earlier incident of terrorism. The three were freed as part of the resolution of the hijackings.

4. On December 1, 1970, members of the ETA kidnapped Eugene Beihl, the honorary West German consul in San Sebastian. They demanded that fifteen Basques charged with murdering a police chief not be executed. Some sort of deal apparently was made; Beihl was released unharmed, and Franco commuted the death sentences that had been given to six of the Basques.

5. On February 22, 1972, Palestinian terrorists hijacked a Lufthansa jet

to Aden, Southern Yemen. The West German government paid $5 million ransom for the plane, the crew, and the passengers.

6. On September 5, 1972, a terrorist squad of the Black September group invaded the Olympic village in Munich and seized nine Israeli athletes, killing two other athletes in the process. The squad demanded a plane to take them to Egypt. There was a shootout at the Munich airport in which all nine athletes and five of the eight members of the Black September squad were killed.

7. On October 6, 1972, Palestinian students briefly held several West Germans hostage in the Federal Republic's consulate in Algiers. They unsuccessfully demanded the release of the surviving members of the Black September squad that had carried out the Munich incident.

8. On October 29, 1972, two hijackers claiming to be members of Black September seized a Lufthansa jet. The hijackers demanded the release of the three surviving terrorists involved in the Munich incident. The West German government gave in and flew the three terrorists to Zagreb, Yugoslavia. The hijacked plane landed at Zagreb, picked up the terrorists, and flew on to Tripoli, Libya, where the plane and its passengers and crew were released.

9. The honorary West German consul in Maracaibo, Venezuela, was kidnapped on November 20, 1973, and released unharmed two days later. The kidnappers were believed to be members of an extreme left group.

10. In March 1975 the Christian Democratic candidate for mayor of West Berlin, Peter Lorenz, was kidnapped by members of the Baader-Meinhof group. He was released after the West German government flew five imprisoned members of the Baader-Meinhof organization to Southern Yemen.

The incidents of terrorism involving demands on private West German parties are as follows:

1. On June 18, 1973, Argentinian guerrillas kidnapped Hans Kurt Gebhardt, a West German clothing manufacturer, and demanded a $100,000 ransom. The ransom was paid, and Gebhardt was released.

2. On December 27, 1973, Thomas Niedermayer, a West German industrialist residing in Ireland, was kidnapped, apparently by a faction of the IRA. Niedermayer has not been heard from since.

(The source for numbers 1 through 9 of the above incidents is Jenkins and Johnson, *Terrorism Chronology*. For further information see the listing in this chronology under the relevant date. Incident 10 is drawn from the *New York Times*, March 3-6, 1975. The two incidents of "private" hostage situations are from the Jenkins and Johnson chronology.)

Table IV in Chapter 6 recorded the number of hostage situations involving Japanese nationals between March 12, 1970, and March 11, 1975. In all there were three incidents in which demands were made on the Japanese government (there were no recorded incidents in this period in which demands were made on Japanese private companies or individuals):

1. On March 31, 1970, members of the Japanese Red Army seized a Japan Air Lines plane and ordered it flown to North Korea. The plane landed at Seoul, let the passengers off, and then flew on to Pyongyang. The North Korean government returned the plane and its crew.

2. On July 20, 1973, a Japan Air Lines 747 was seized by one Japanese and three Arab hijackers. A fifth hijacker, a woman from Latin America with a Peruvian passport, was killed shortly after the takeover when a grenade she was holding accidentally went off. The woman was apparently the leader, because after her death the other terrorists became confused. The plane finally landed at Dubai. Japanese officials arrived to negotiate, but the hijackers refused to talk to them. Instead they ordered the plane to Benghazi, where they released the passengers and crew and then destroyed the aircraft with explosives.

3. On January 31, 1974, two members of the Japanese Red Army and two members of the PFLP, after unsuccessfully attempting to destroy a Shell oil refinery in Singapore, seized a ferryboat and held three hostages. On February 6 a five-member PFLP squad invaded the Japanese embassy in Kuwait, capturing twelve hostages. They demanded that the Japanese government supply an airliner to bring their comrades in Singapore to Kuwait. The Japanese complied, and the four terrorists on the ferryboat were flown to Kuwait. The five PFLP members were picked up, and the plane flew on to Southern Yemen, where the terrorists received asylum.

(All of the above information about these incidents is from Jenkins and Johnson, *Terrorism Chronology.*)

Table IV in Chapter 6 recorded the number of hostage situations involving American nationals between August 10, 1970, and August 9, 1975. In all there were twenty-one incidents of "nonprivate" kidnappings and thirteen incidents of "private" kidnappings. The nonprivate kidnappings were as follows:

1. In the September 1970 PFLP hijackings there were a number of Americans held hostage (a Pan Am 747 and a TWA 707 were among the planes hijacked).

2. On October 22, 1970, a Costa Rican airliner with four Americans on board was hijacked to Cuba. The hijackers held the Americans hostage and demanded the release of four Nicaraguan guerrillas held in Costa Rica. The guerrillas were flown to Cuba, and the hostages were released.

3. In November 1970 there was an unsuccessful attempt to kidnap Douglas MacArthur II, the American ambassador to Iran.

4. On February 15, 1971, the Turkish People's Liberation Army (TPLA) kidnapped James Finlay, a U.S. Air Force security policeman, and held him briefly. Finlay was released unharmed.

5. On March 4, 1971, the TPLA seized four American servicemen who were stationed near Ankara. The TPLA demanded the payment of a ransom of 400,000 Turkish lira and the publication of a manifesto attacking American imperialism. The Turkish government refused to give in. The four servicemen were released unharmed on March 8.

6. On January 23, 1973, Clinton E. Knox, the American ambassador to Haiti, and American Consul General Ward L. Christensen were seized and held hostage in the ambassador's residence by three members of an anti-Duvalier group. The kidnappers eventually released their hostages in return for twelve prisoners and a $70,000 ransom.

7. On March 1, 1973, a Black September squad took over the Saudi Arabian embassy in Khartoum and held a number of diplomats hostage, including the American ambassador to the Sudan, Cleo A. Noel, and his deputy chief of mission, Curtis Moore. The terrorists demanded the release of Palestinian prisoners in Israel and Jordan and the release of Sirhan Sirhan, the killer of Senator Robert Kennedy. At a news conference on March 2 President Nixon said that the United States would "not pay blackmail." On the evening of March 2 Noel and Moore were killed along with Belgian Chargé Guy Eid. The terrorists surrendered on March 3.

8. On May 4, 1973, the American consul general in Guadalajara, Terrance G. Leonhardy, was kidnapped by Mexican terrorists. He was released after the Mexican government flew thirty prisoners to Cuba and published the terrorists' communiqué and Leonhardy's wife raised an $800,000 ransom.

9. On October 18, 1973, a squad of five terrorists from a group calling itself the Lebanese Socialist Revolutionary Organization raided a Bank of America office in Beirut and held forty people hostage, including some Americans. The group's demands were for $10 million to finance the Arab war effort (the Yom Kippur war was going on at the time of this incident) and for the United States to stop helping Israel in this war. The Lebanese police and army stormed the bank. One American hostage, John Crawford Maxwell, was killed in the course of the event.

10. On March 25, 1974, John Patterson, American vice-consul in Hermosillo, Mexico, was kidnapped by Mexican terrorists. The case is unclear; there were reports of ransom demands of some sort. The family attempted to comply with the ransom demands but were not successful. Patterson's body was found 107 days after the kidnapping in a spot near Hermosillo.

11. On April 12, 1974, Alfred Laun, head of the United States Information Agency branch in Cordoba, Argentina, was kidnapped by the ERP. He was

wounded in the course of the kidnapping and was released on April 13, apparently because of the seriousness of his wounds.

12. On April 23, 1974, the Pattani Liberation Front, a Muslim separatist movement in southern Thailand, kidnapped two American women missionaries. They demanded that the United States terminate aid to the Thai government.

13. On May 27, 1974, a Dutch and an American nurse were kidnapped by the Eritrean Liberation Front in Ghinda, Ethiopia. The Dutch nurse was killed. The American nurse was released on June 22, 1974, after negotiations between the ELF and a missionary group. The ELF apparently wanted to protest against American involvement in Eritrea.

14. In September 1974 U.S. Information Agency officer Barbara Hutchinson and several other individuals were seized and held hostage by terrorists at the agency's offices in the Dominican Republic. The terrorists demanded the release of captured comrades. The government of the Dominican Republic refused to give in to the terrorists' demands that several of their captured comrades be freed but eventually allowed the kidnappers to seek asylum in Panama in exchange for releasing Hutchinson and the other hostages.

15. In February 1975 American consular agent in Argentina John Egan was kidnapped from his home. The demands of the terrorists were not met, and Egan was killed.

16. In April 1975 John McKay, a Drug Enforcement Agency official, was detained by Palestinian guerrillas at the Sabra refugee camp in Beirut. He was released after two days.

17. In May 1975 Foreign Service Officer Michael Konner was abducted in Beirut by a group of Palestinians. He was released after being held for 14 hours.

18. In June 1975 U.S. Army Colonel Ernest Morgan was kidnapped in Lebanon by a faction of the PFLP. The terrorists demanded that the American government distribute food in a slum area of Beirut. Morgan was released after an unknown source distributed food.

19. On July 14, 1975, James Harrell and Steven Campbell, employees of Collins International Service Company stationed at the American base in Asmara, Ethiopia, were kidnapped by the Popular Liberation Front, an Eritrean separatist group. Harrell and Campbell were released on May 3, 1976.

20. On August 2, 1975, Constance Stansky, an American national, was seized in Lebanon by an unidentified Palestinian group. She was released 11 days later.

21. On August 4, 1975, three American citizens plus U.S. Consul Robert

Stebbins and fifty other people of various nationalities were seized and held hostage at the American embassy in Kuala Lumpur by five members of the Japanese Red Army. The hostages were released after the Japanese government gave in to the terrorists' demand that five Red Army members being held in Japan be released. All ten terrorists were flown to Libya on a Japan Air Lines plane.

(There are two basic sources for the above incidents. The first is Jenkins and Johnson's *Terrorism Chronology*. The second is two sets of State Department chronologies: *Chronology of Attacks Upon Non-Official American Citizens* and *Chronology of Significant Terrorist Incidents Involving U.S. Diplomatic/Official Personnel*. The latter two chronologies were compiled by the office of the special assistant to the Secretary of State for combatting terrorism. They are in the form of an unpublished manuscript. Incidents 1 through 10 and 13 are from the Jenkins and Johnson chronology; incidents 11 through 12 and 14 through 21 are from the State Department's chronologies.)

In Table IV in Chapter 6 it was reported that in the period August 10, 1970, to August 9, 1975, there were a total of thirteen incidents of political kidnappings involving American nationals in which the major focus of the demands was on private companies or on individuals. The following is a list of these incidents.

1. On December 27, 1972, an ITT executive named Vicente Russo was kidnapped by Argentinian terrorists. He was released on December 29. The size of the ransom was undisclosed.

2. On March 28, 1973, Gerardo Scalmazzi, manager of the Rosario, Argentina, branch of the First National Bank of Boston, was kidnapped by Argentinian terrorists. He was released after the bank paid between $500,000 and $1 million in ransom.

3. On April 2, 1973, Argentinian terrorists kidnapped Anthony R. DaCruz, a business manager for Eastman Kodak's Argentinian operations. He was released in return for a $1.5 million ransom.

4. On May 21, 1973, Oscar Castel, manager of a Coca-Cola bottling plant in Cordoba, Argentina, was kidnapped by a group of terrorists. He was released after the payment of a $100,000 ransom.

5. On June 18, 1973, members of the Argentinian ERP kidnapped John R. Thompson, president of Firestone Tire and Rubber Company's subsidiary in Argentina. He was released following payment of a $3 million ransom.

6. On October 4, 1973, Willis Leon Dotsun and Rene Francis Kast, American employees of the Frontino Gold Mines in Colombia, were kidnapped by the Ejército de Liberación Nacional (ELN), or National Libera-

tion Army, a Colombian terrorist group. The kidnappers demanded a $168,990 ransom. The company tried to pay the ransom, but Colombian authorities seized the money when an attempt was made to get in contact with the kidnappers. The Colombian army rescued the two men on March 7, 1974.

7. On October 25, 1973, David Wilkie, Jr., president of Amoco's Argentinian subsidiary, was kidnapped in Buenos Aires. He was released after the payment of a $3.5 million ransom.

8. On December 6, 1973, Victor Samuelson, an American executive of the Exxon Company's Argentinian branch, was kidnapped by the ERP. He was freed after the payment of a $14.2 million ransom.

9. On December 21, 1973, Charles R. Hayes, an engineer with the firm of A. G. McKee and Company, was kidnapped in Argentina. He was released following the payment of an undisclosed ransom.

10. On January 4, 1974, Douglas G. Roberts, the director of the Pepsi-Cola Company in Argentina, was kidnapped by terrorists. He was released following the payment of an undisclosed ransom.

11. On March 26, 1974, the Eritrean Liberation Front kidnapped five employees, two Canadians and three Americans, of Tenneco, Inc., an American-based oil company. The individuals were seized when a Tenneco helicopter made a landing in ELF-controlled territory in Eritrea. The Canadian pilot of the helicopter was released on June 27, 1974. The remaining four hostages were released on September 11, 1974, after six months of negotiations between Tenneco officials and the ELF.

12. On May 19, 1975, members of the People's Revolutionary party, a Zaire-based guerrilla group, kidnapped three Americans (Barbara Smuts, Connie Hunter, and Kenneth Steven Smith) and a Dutch woman (Emilie Bergmann) from an animal research center in Tanzania and took them into Zaire. All of the students were from Stanford University. The students were released after their parents paid a $400,000 ransom.

13. On August 5, 1975, Donald Cooper, a Sears Roebuck executive, was abducted from his home in Bogotá, Colombia, by a group of eight terrorists. After 3 months of negotiations between Sears and the terrorists, Cooper was released unharmed on November 2, 1975. It is not known what ransom arrangements, if any, were made.

(The source for these incidents is the Jenkins and Johnson *Terrorism Chronology* and the Department of State's *Chronology of Attacks Upon Non-Official Americans*. The accounts of incidents 1 through 5, 7 through 8, and 10 are taken from the Jenkins and Johnson chronology. The accounts of incidents 6, 9, and 11 through 13 are from the State Department's chronology.)

appendix III

UNITED NATIONS
DOCUMENTS ON
TERRORISM

U.S. DRAFT CONVENTION FOR THE
PREVENTION AND PUNISHMENT OF CERTAIN
ACTS OF INTERNATIONAL TERRORISM*

THE STATES PARTIES TO THIS CONVENTION

RECALLING United Nations General Assembly Resolution 2625 (XXV) proclaiming principles of international law concerning friendly relations and co-operation among States in accordance with the Charter of the United Nations;

CONSIDERING that this resolution provides that every State has the duty to refrain from organizing, instigating, assisting or participating in terrorist acts in another State or acquiescing in organized activities within its territory directed towards the commission of such acts;

CONSIDERING the common danger posed by the spread of terrorist acts across national boundaries;

CONSIDERING that civilians must be protected from terrorist acts;

AFFIRMING that effective measures to control international terrorism are urgently needed and require international as well as national action;

HAVE AGREED AS FOLLOWS:

ARTICLE 1

1. Any person who unlawfully kills, causes serious bodily harm or

*The text of this convention comes from *Department of State Bulletin,* October 16, 1972, pp. 431-433.

kidnaps another person, attempts to commit such an act, or participates as an accomplice of a person who commits or attempts to commit any such act, commits an offense of international significance if the act:

(a) is committed or takes effect outside the territory of a State of which the alleged offender is a national; and

(b) is committed or takes effect:

(i) outside the territory of the State against which the act is directed, or

(ii) within the territory of the State against which the act is directed and the alleged offender knows or has reason to know that a person against whom the act is directed is not a national of that State; and

(c) is committed neither by nor against a member of the Armed Forces of a State in the course of military hostilities; and

(d) is intended to damage the interests of or obtain concessions from a State or an international organization.

2. For the purposes of this Convention:

(a) An "international organization" means an international intergovernmental organization.

(b) An "alleged offender" means a person as to whom there are grounds to believe that he has committed one or more of the offenses of international significance set forth in this Article.

(c) The "territory" of a State includes all territory under the jurisdiction or administration of the State.

ARTICLE 2

Each State Party undertakes to make the offenses set forth in Article 1 punishable by severe penalties.

ARTICLE 3

A State Party in whose territory an alleged offender is found shall, if it does not extradite him, submit, without exception whatsoever and without undue delay, the case to its competent authorities for the purpose of prosecution, through proceedings in accordance with the laws of that State.

ARTICLE 4

1. Each State Party shall take such measures as may be necessary to establish its jurisdiction over the offenses set forth in Article 1:

(a) when the offense is committed in its territory, or

(b) when the offense is committed by its national.

2. Each State Party shall likewise take such measures as may be necessary to establish its jurisdiction over the offenses set forth in Article 1 in the case

where an alleged offender is present in its territory and the State does not extradite him to any of the States mentioned in Paragraph 1 of this Article.

3. This Convention does not exclude any criminal jurisdiction exercised in accordance with national law.

A State Party in which one or more of the offenses set forth in Article 1 have been committed shall, if it has reason to believe an alleged offender has fled from its territory, communicate to all other State Parties all the pertinent facts regarding the offense committed and all available information regarding the identity of the alleged offender.

1. The State Party in whose territory an alleged offender is found shall take appropriate measures under its internal law so as to ensure his presence for prosecution or extradition. Such measures shall be immediately notified to the States mentioned in Article 4, Paragraph 1, and all other interested States.

2. Any person regarding whom the measures referred to in Paragraph 1 of this Article are being taken shall be entitled to communicate immediately with the nearest appropriate representative of the State of which he is a national and to be visited by a representative of that State.

1. To the extent that the offenses set forth in Article 1 are not listed as extraditable offenses in any extradition treaty existing between States Parties they shall be deemed to have been included as such therein. States Parties undertake to include those offenses as extraditable offenses in every future extradition treaty to be concluded between them.

2. If a State Party which makes extradition conditional on the existence of a treaty receives a request for extradition from another State Party with whom it has no extradition treaty, it may, if it decides to extradite, consider the present articles as the legal basis for extradition in respect of the offenses. Extradition shall be subject to the provisions of the law of the requested State.

3. States Parties which do not make extradition conditional upon the existence of a treaty shall recognize the offenses as extraditable offenses between themselves subject to the provisions of the law of the requested State.

4. Each of the offenses shall be treated, for the purpose of extradition between States Parties, as if it has been committed not only in the place in which it occurred but also in the territories of the States required to establish their jurisdiction in accordance with Article 4, Paragraph 1(b).

5. An extradition request from the State in which the offenses were committed shall have priority over other such requests if received by the State Party in whose territory the alleged offender has been found within thirty days after the communication required in Paragraph 1 of Article 6 has been made.

ARTICLE 8

Any person regarding whom proceedings are being carried out in connection with any of the offenses set forth in Article 1 shall be guaranteed fair treatment at all stages of the proceedings.

ARTICLE 9

The statutory limitation as to the time within which prosecution may be instituted for the offenses set forth in Article 1 shall be, in each State Party, that fixed for the most serious crimes under its internal law.

ARTICLE 10

1. State Parties shall, in accordance with international and national law, endeavor to take all practicable measures for the purpose of preventing the offenses set forth in Article 1.

2. Any State Party having reason to believe that one of the offenses set forth in Article 1 may be committed shall, in accordance with its national law, furnish any relevant information in its possession to those States which it believes would be the States mentioned in Article 4, Paragraph 1, if any such offense were committed.

ARTICLE 11

1. States Parties shall afford one another the greatest measure of assistance in connection with criminal proceedings brought in respect of the offenses set forth in Article 1, including the supply of all evidence at their disposal necessary for the proceedings.

2. The provisions of Paragraph 1 of this Article shall not affect obligations concerning mutual assistance embodied in any other treaty.

States Parties shall consult together for the purpose of considering and implementing such other cooperative measures as may seem useful for the carrying out of the purposes of this Convention.

In any case in which one or more of the Geneva Conventions of August 12, 1949, or any other convention concerning the law of armed conflict is applicable, such conventions shall, if in conflict with any provision of this Convention, take precedence. In particular:

(a) nothing in this Convention shall make an offense of any act which is permissible under the Geneva Convention Relative to the Protection of Civilian Persons in Time of War or any other international law applicable in armed conflicts; and

(b) nothing in this Convention shall deprive any person of prisoner of war status if entitled to such status under the Geneva Convention Relative to the Treatment of Prisoners of War or any other applicable convention concerning respect for human rights in armed conflicts.

In any case in which the Convention on Offenses and Certain Other Acts Committed on Board Aircraft, the Convention for the Suppression of Unlawful Seizure of Aircraft, the Convention for the Suppression of Unlawful Acts Against the Safety of Civil Aviation, the Convention to Prevent and Punish the Acts of Terrorism Taking the Form of Crimes Against Persons and Related Extortion that Are of International Significance, or any other convention which has or may be concluded concerning the protection of civil aviation, diplomatic agents and other internationally protected persons, is applicable, such convention shall, if in conflict with any provision of this Convention, take precedence.

Nothing in this Convention shall derogate from any obligations of the Parties under the United Nations Charter.

1. Any dispute between the Parties arising out of the application or interpretation of the present articles that is not settled through negotiation may

be brought by any State party to the dispute before a Conciliation Commission to be constituted in accordance with the provisions of this Article by the giving of written notice to the other State or States party to the dispute and to the Secretary-General of the United Nations.

2. A Conciliation Commission will be composed of three members. One member shall be appointed by each party to the dispute. If there is more than one party on either side of the dispute they shall jointly appoint a member of the Conciliation Commission. These two appointments shall be made within two months of the written notice referred to in Paragraph 1. The third member, the Chairman, shall be chosen by the other two members.

3. If either side has failed to appoint its members within the time limit referred to in Paragraph 2, the Secretary-General of the United Nations shall appoint such member within a further period of two months. If no agreement is reached on the choice of the chairman within five months of the written notice referred to in Paragraph 1, the Secretary-General shall within the further period of one month appoint as the Chairman a qualified jurist who is not a national of any State party to the dispute.

4. Any vacancy shall be filled in the same manner as the original appointment was made.

5. The Commission shall establish its own rules of procedure and shall reach its decisions and recommendations by a majority vote. It shall be competent to ask any organ that is authorized by or in accordance with the Charter of the United Nations to request an advisory opinion from the International Court of Justice to make such a request regarding the interpretation or application of the present articles.

6. If the Commission is unable to obtain an agreement among the parties on a settlement of the dispute within six months of its initial meeting, it shall prepare as soon as possible a report of its proceedings and transmit it to the parties and to the depositary. The report shall include the Commission's conclusions upon the facts and questions of law and the recommendations it has submitted to the parties in order to facilitate a settlement of the dispute. The six months time limit may be extended by decision of the Commission.

7. This Article is without prejudice to provisions concerning the settlement of disputes contained in international agreements in force between States.

UNITED NATIONS GENERAL ASSEMBLY
Twenty-seventh session   A/C.6/L.851
SIXTH   COMMITTEE   25 September 1972
Agenda item 92   ORIGINAL: ENGLISH

MEASURES TO PREVENT INTERNATIONAL TERRORISM
WHICH ENDANGERS OR TAKES INNOCENT HUMAN LIVES
OR JEOPARDIZES FUNDAMENTAL FREEDOMS, AND STUDY
OF THE UNDERLYING CAUSES OF THOSE FORMS OF TERROR-
ISM AND ACTS OF VIOLENCE WHICH LIE IN MISERY, FRUS-
TRATION, GRIEVANCE AND DESPAIR AND WHICH CAUSE
SOME PEOPLE TO SACRIFICE HUMAN LIVES, INCLUDING
THEIR OWN, IN AN ATTEMPT TO EFFECT RADICAL CHANGES

United States of America: draft resolution
The General Assembly,

Gravely concerned by the increasing frequency of serious acts of international terrorism, inflicting injury and death to innocent persons and inflam-
ing relations between peoples and States,

Deploring the tragic, unwarranted and unnecessary loss of innocent
human lives from acts of international terrorism,

Recognizing that the continuation of international terrorism poses a grave
threat to the safety and reliability of modern communications between
States, including in particular international civil aviation and diplomatic
intercourse,

Recognizing that Governments have the responsibility to take appropriate steps to assure that all foreign diplomats engaging in normal pursuits
and all foreign nationals travelling, visiting or residing abroad are afforded
full legal protection against bodily harm or the threat thereof,

Noting the constructive initiative of the Secretary-General to place an
item on international terrorism before the General Assembly,

Recalling the General Assembly's Declaration on Principles of International Law concerning Friendly Relations and Co-operation among States
in accordance with the Charter of the United Nations, in particular its
statement that

"Every State has the duty to refrain from organizing, instigating,
assisting or participating in acts of civil strife or terrorist acts in
another State or acquiescing in organized activities within its

territory directed towards the commission of such acts, when the acts referred to in the present paragraph involve a threat or use of force."

1. *Calls upon* all States as a matter of urgency to become parties to and implement the following international conventions:

   (a) Convention on Offences and Certain Other Acts Committed on Board Aircraft, signed at Tokyo on 14 September 1963;
   (b) Convention for the Suppression of Unlawful Seizure of Aircraft, signed at The Hague on 15 December 1970;
   (c) Convention for the Suppression of Unlawful Acts Against the Safety of Civil Aviation, signed at Montreal on 23 September 1971;

2. *Requests* the International Civil Aviation Organization to pursue as a matter of urgency the drafting of a convention on arrangements for enforcement of principles and obligations embodied in the Tokyo, Hague and Montreal Conventions with a view to the calling of a plenipotentiary conference without delay;

3. *Urges* all States to take immediate steps to prevent the use of their territory or resources to aid, encourage, or give sanctuary to those persons involved in directing, supporting or participating in acts of international terrorism;

4. *Calls upon* all States urgently to take all necessary measures within their jurisdiction and in co-operation with other States to deter and prevent acts of international terrorism and to take effective measures to deal with those who perpetrate such acts;

5. *Strongly recommends* that Member Governments establish procedures for the exchange of information and data on the plans, activities and movements of terrorists, in order to strengthen the capability of Governments to prevent and suppress acts of international terrorism and to prosecute and punish those perpetrating such acts;

6. *Calls upon* all States to become parties to a convention on the prevention and punishment of crimes against diplomatic agents and other internationally protected persons based on the draft articles prepared by the International Law Commission;

7. *Decides* to convene a plenipotentiary conference in early 1973 to consider the adoption of a convention on the prevention and punishment of international terrorism and requests the Secretary-General to transmit to Member States for their consideration the texts of proposed draft articles on this subject submitted to the General Assembly;

8. *Recommends* urgent efforts by all members to address the political problems which may, in some instances, provide a pretext for acts of international terrorism.

UNITED NATIONS GENERAL ASSEMBLY
Twenty-seventh session   A/C.6/L.879/Rev.1
SIXTH COMMITTEE   8 December 1972
Agenda item 92   ORIGINAL: ENGLISH

MEASURES TO PREVENT INTERNATIONAL TERRORISM
WHICH ENDANGERS OR TAKES INNOCENT HUMAN LIVES
OR JEOPARDIZES FUNDAMENTAL FREEDOMS, AND STUDY
OF THE UNDERLYING CAUSES OF THOSE FORMS OF TER-
RORISM AND ACTS OF VIOLENCE WHICH LIE IN MISERY,
FRUSTRATION, GRIEVANCE AND DESPAIR AND WHICH
CAUSE SOME PEOPLE TO SACRIFICE HUMAN LIVES, INCLUD-
ING THEIR OWN, IN AN ATTEMPT TO EFFECT RADICAL
CHANGES

*Austria, Australia, Belgium, Canada, Costa Rica, Guatemala,
Honduras, Iran, Italy, Japan, Luxemburg, New Zealand, Nicaragua
and United Kingdom of Great Britain and Norther Ireland: revised
draft resolution*

The General Assembly,
Reaffirming the faith of the peoples of the United Nations in fundamental
rights and in the dignity and worth of the human person and their determination to practice tolerance and live together in peace with one another as
good neighbors,
Expressing its deep concern at the continuous increase in acts of international terrorism which endanger or take innocent human lives or jeopardize
fundamental freedoms as well as at the underlying causes of those forms of
terrorism and acts of violence which lie in misery, frustration, grievance
and despair and which cause some people to sacrifice human lives, including
their own, in an attempt to effect radical changes,
Reaffirming the principle of equal rights and self-determination contained
in the United Nations Charter and elaborated in the Declaration of Principles of International Law concerning Friendly Relations and Co-operation
among States in accordance with the Charter of the United Nations [resolu-
tion 2625 (XXV)],

Affirming that nothing in this resolution shall be construed as enlarging or diminishing in any way the scope of the provision of the Charter concerning cases in which the use of force is lawful,

Recognizing that, at all times, a distinction must be drawn in every form of human conflict between, on one hand, the right to resort to force and, on the other, the means used in pursuance of this right, certain means being illegitimate in all circumstances,

Considering as intolerable to the international community acts of international terrorism, which often not only inflict injury or death on innocent persons even beyond areas of tension, but also affect the interests of one or more States and undermine the very foundations of international communications, diplomacy and order, which are essential for international peace and the welfare of peoples everywhere,

Convinced of the need for urgent new measures to prevent the spread of international terrorism, especially to countries or individuals not parties to the conflict concerned, and also for an intensified search for solutions which would remove the underlying causes,

1. *Condemns* acts of international terrorism, particularly those resulting in the loss of innocent lives;

2. *Calls upon* all States urgently to take all appropriate measures at the national level for the fulfillment of their obligations to refrain from organizing, instigating, assisting or participating in such acts of international terrorism or acquiescing in organized activities within their territories directed towards the commission of such acts;

3. *Urges* Member States to co-operate more effectively with each other for the purpose of ensuring full protection of the public against acts of international terrorism including, in conformity with their national legislation and through agreed international machinery, the exchange of information and data necessary to strengthen the capability of Governments to prevent and suppress such acts and prosecute or extradite those perpetrating them;

4. *Calls upon* all States as a matter or urgency to become parties to and implement the relevant international Conventions, particularly those concerning unlawful acts committed on board or against aircraft and the safety of civil aviation;

5. *Requests* the International Law Commission to draft, with the highest priority, a Convention on measures to prevent international terrorism, having particular regard to violence affecting countries or individuals not parties to the conflict concerned or directed against common means of international transportation and communications, for submission to the

twenty-eighth session of the General Assembly with a view to its adoption at a Conference of Plenipotentiaries to take place at the earliest practical date;

6. *Requests further* Member States to assist the International Civil Aviation Organization (ICAO) to pursue as a matter or urgency its endeavours to reach agreement among States on appropriate multilateral procedures within the framework of ICAO aimed at eliminating the threat to the safety and security of civil aviation;

7. *Decides* to establish an *Ad Hoc* Committee consisting of . . . members, to be appointed by the President of the General Assembly, keeping in mind the principle of equitable geographical distribution, and to be represented by persons having the appropriate expert knowledge, with the task of studying the underlying causes of those forms of terrorism and acts of violence which lie in misery, frustration, grievance and despair and which cause some people to sacrifice human lives, including their own, in an attempt to effect radical changes and of submitting a report, with suggestions as appropriate, to the twenty-eighth session of the General Assembly;

8. *Requests* the Secretary-General to seek views and comments of Member States and to provide such views and comments to the International Law Commission and to the *Ad Hoc* Committee by 31 March 1973 with all documentation relating to the discussion of this item at the present twenty-seventh session;

9. *Decides* to include in the provisional agenda of the twenty-eighth session of the General Assembly an item entitled "Measures to prevent international terrorism which endangers or takes innocent human lives or jeopardizes fundamental freedoms and study of the underlying causes of those forms of terrorism and acts of violence which lie in misery, frustration, grievance and despair and which cause some people to sacrifice human lives, including their own, in an attempt to effect radical changes."

UNITED NATIONS GENERAL ASSEMBLY
Twenty-seventh session   A/C.6/L.880/Rev.1
SIXTH COMMITTEE   8 December 1972
Agenda item 92   ORIGINAL: ENGLISH

MEASURES TO PREVENT INTERNATIONAL TERRORISM
WHICH ENDANGERS OR TAKES INNOCENT HUMAN LIVES
OR JEOPARDIZES FUNDAMENTAL FREEDOMS, AND STUDY
OF THE UNDERLYING CAUSES OF THESE FORMS OF TERROR-
ISM AND ACTS OF VIOLENCE WHICH LIE IN MISERY, FRUS-
TRATION, GRIEVANCE AND DESPAIR, AND WHICH CAUSE
SOME PEOPLE TO SACRIFICE HUMAN LIVES, INCLUDING
THEIR OWN, IN AN ATTEMPT TO EFFECT RADICAL CHANGES

Afghanistan, Algeria, Cameroon, Chad, Congo, Equatorial Guinea,
Guyana, India, Kenya, Madagascar, Mauritania, Mali, Sudan,
Yugoslavia, Zambia: revised draft resolution
The General Assembly,
Deeply perturbed over acts of international terrorism which are oc-
curring with increasing frequency and which take a toll of innocent human
lives,
Recognizing the importance of international co-operation in devising
measures to effectively prevent their occurrence and of studying their
underlying causes with a view to finding just and peaceful solutions as
quickly as possible,
Recalling the Declaration on Principles of International Law concerning
Friendly Relations and Co-operation among States in accordance with the
Charter of the United Nations,
1. *Expresses* deep concern over increasing acts of violence which endanger or take innocent human lives or jeopardize fundamental freedoms;
2. *Urges* States to devote their immediate attention to finding just and
peaceful solutions to the underlying causes which give rise to such acts of
violence;
3. *Reaffirms* the inalienable right to self-determination and independence
of all peoples under colonial and racist régimes and other forms of alien
domination and upholds the legitimacy of their struggle, in particular the
struggle of national liberation movements, in accordance with the purposes

and principles of the Charter and the relevant resolutions of the organs of the United Nations;

4. *Condemns* the continuation of repressive and terrorist acts by colonial racist and alien régimes in denying peoples their legitimate right to self-determination and independence and other forms of human rights and fundamental freedoms;

5. *Invites* States to become parties to the existing international conventions which relate to various aspects of the problem of international terrorism;

6. *Invites* States to take all appropriate measures at the national level, with a view to the speedy and final elimination of the problem, bearing in mind the provisions of paragraph 3;

7. *Invites* States to consider the subject matter urgently and submit observations to the Secretary-General by 1 June 1973, including concrete proposals for finding an effective solution to the problem;

8. *Requests* the Secretary-General to transmit an analytical study of the observations of States under paragraph 7 to the *ad hoc* Committee to be established under paragraph 9;

9. *Decides* to establish an *Ad Hoc* Committee consisting of thirty-five members, to be appointed by the President of the General Assembly, bearing in mind the principle of equitable geographical representation;

10. *Requests* the *Ad Hoc* Committee to consider the observations of States under paragraph 7 and submit its report with recommendations for possible co-operation for the speedy elimination of the problem, bearing in mind the provisions of paragraph 3, to the twenty-eighth session of the General Assembly;

11. *Requests* the Secretary-General to provide the *Ad Hoc* Committee with the necessary facilities and services;

12. *Decides* to include the item in the provisional agenda of the twenty-eighth session of the General Assembly.

appendix IV
INDIVIDUALS INTERVIEWED
AND CONSULTED
FOR THIS BOOK

People knowledgeable about revolutionary movements (the numbers refer to interview numbers used in the footnotes):

Palestinian Movement

1. **Galia Golan**—Professor of political science at the Hebrew University of Jerusalem.
2. **Shamon Shamir**—professor of Middle Eastern studies at Tel Aviv University.
3. **Gavriel Ben-Dor**—professor of Middle Eastern studies at the University of Haifa.
4. **Rehoboam Ze'ev**—assistant to the prime minister of Israel for terrorism.
5. **Bernard Johns**—American foreign service officer at the American consulate-general in Jerusalem.
6. **William Kirby**—American foreign service officer at the American embassy in Tel Aviv.

Zionist Underground

7. **Nathan Yalin-Mor**—former high official in the Freedom Fighters of Israel (the Stern Group).
8. **Eli Tavin**—former high official in the Irgun Zvai Leumi.

Tupamaros

9. **Geoffrey Jackson**—former British ambassador to Uruguay.

Irish Republican Movement

10. **Sean Cronin**—former chief of staff of the Irish Republican Army.
11. **Joseph Cahill**—vice-president of the Provisional Sinn Fein.
12. **Sean Keenan**—editor of the Republican newspaper *An Phoblacht.*
13. Member of the Belfast Provisional Sinn Fein.
14. Member of the Belfast Provisional Sinn Fein.
15. **Sean Brady**—information officer of the Provisional Sinn Fein.
16. **Tomas MacGiolla**—president of the Official Sinn Fein.
17. **Sean Garland**—vice-president of the Official Sinn Fein.
18. **Seamus Costello**—president of the Irish Republican Socialist Party (IRSP).
19. **John Haslam**—chief British information officer for Ulster.

Ulster Protestant Paramilitaries

20. **Andrew Tyrie**—commander of the Ulster Defense Association.
21. **Sarah Nelson**—doctoral candidate doing a dissertation on the Protestant Loyalists in Ulster.

People knowledgeable about American policy toward international terrorism:

22. Member of the American delegation to the United Nations.
23. **Robert Myers**—foreign service officer serving under the special assistant to the Secretary of State for combatting terrorism.
24. Foreign service officer serving under the special assistant to the Secretary of State for combatting terrorism.
25. **Allison Palmer**—Foreign service officer active in the professional organization of the foreign service.
26. **Robert Feary**—special assistant to the Secretary of State for combatting terrorism.
27. **Franklin Crawford**—foreign service officer serving with the United Nations desk in the Department of State.
28. **Theodore Taylor**—expert on nuclear energy.
29. **Norman Rasmussen**—MIT expert on nuclear energy.
30. Foreign service officer specializing in international legal affairs.
31. **Daniel Moynihan**—former United States ambassador to the United Nations.
32. Staff member of the office of the special assistant to the Secretary of State for combatting terrorism.
33. **Sean Holly**—former American labor attaché in Guatemala.
34. Foreign service officer serving with the Department of State's office of security.

35. Foreign service officer active in the professional organization of the foreign service.

People knowledgeable about Israel's reprisal policy:

36. **Hissam Atassi**—official at the Israeli consulate in New York City.
37. **Dan Horowitz**—professor of political science at the Hebrew University of Jerusalem.
38. Official in the Israeli ministry of foreign affairs.
39. Official in the Israeli ministry of foreign affairs.
40. Official in the Israeli ministry of foreign affairs.
41. **Uri Reychav**—official in the Israeli ministry of defense.
42. **Ze'ev Schiff**—military correspondent for the Israeli newspaper *Ha'aretz*.
43. **Yehezkel Dror**—official in the Israeli ministry of defense.
44. **Daniel Shimshoni**—director of the Israeli think tank Stratis.
45. **Yair Evron**—Israeli expert on Middle Eastern affairs.

General background on terrorism *(These individuals were not interviewed; the author attended a "backgrounder" they gave at the Department of State in March 1976):*

46. **Robert Moss**—British expert on terrorism.
47. **Brian Jenkins**—RAND Corporation expert on terrorism.

BIBLIOGRAPHY

I. Literature on Revolutionary Movements

A. THE MIDDLE EAST

"Arafat's Speech to the United Nations." *Journal of Palestine Studies,* Vol. IV, No. 2 (Winter 1975), pp. 181-192.

Begin, Menachem. *The Revolt.* Jerusalem: Steimatzky's Agency Limited, 1972.

Bell, J. Bowyer. "Assassination in International Politics: Lord Moyne, Count Bernadotte, and the Lehi." *International Studies Quarterly,* Vol. XVI, No. 1 (March 1972), pp. 59-82.

_____. *Terror Out of Zion.* New York: St. Martin's Press, 1977.

Blechman, Barry. *The Consequences of Israeli Reprisals: An Assessment.* Ph.D. dissertation, Georgetown University, 1971.

_____. "The Impact of Israel's Reprisals on Behavior of the Bordering Arab Nations Directed at Israel." *Journal of Conflict Resolution,* Vol. XVI, No. 2 (June 1972), pp. 155-181.

Cooley, John. *Green March, Black September.* London: Frank Cass, 1973.

Dobson, Christopher. *Black September.* New York: Macmillan Publishing Company, Inc., 1974.

Grivas, George. *Memoirs of General Grivas.* New York: Frederick A. Praeger, 1965.

Harkabi, Y. *Palestinians and Israel.* Jerusalem: Keter Publishing House, 1974.

_____. *Fedayeen Action and Arab Strategy.* London: International Institute for Strategic Studies, 1968.

Khaled, Leila. *My People Shall Live.* London: Hodden and Staughton, 1973.
Lewis, Bernard. "The Palestinians and the PLO." *Commentary,* Vol. 59, No. 1 (January 1975), pp. 32-48.
Maksoud, Clovis. *Palestine Lives.* Beirut: Palestine Research Center, 1973.
Ma'oz, Moshe. *Soviet and Chinese Relations with the Palestinian Guerrilla Organization.* Jerusalem: The Hebrew University, Jerusalem Papers on Peace Problems, 1974.
Quandt, William B., Jabber, Fuad, and Ann Mosely Lesch. *The Politics of Palestinian Nationalism.* Berkeley, California: University of California Press, 1972.
Rondot, Pierre. "Palestine: Peace Talks and Militancy." *World Today,* Vol. XXX, No. 9 (September 1974), pp. 379-387.
Rothstein, Raphael and Ze'ev Schiff. *Fedayeen.* New York: David McKay Company, 1972.
Sharabi, Hisham. *Palestine Guerrillas: Their Credibility and Effectiveness.* Beirut: The Institute for Palestine Studies, 1970.
Tophaven, Rolf. *Fedayin.* Munich: Bernard and Graefe Verlag fur Wehrwessen, 1975.
Yaari, Ehud. *Strike Terror.* New York: Sabra Books, 1970.

B. AFRICA

Bell, J. Bowyer. "Endemic Insurgency and International Order: The Eritrean Experience." *Orbis,* Vol. XVIII, No. 2 (Summer 1974), pp. 427-450.
Duchene, François (ed.). *Conflicts in Africa.* London: International Institute for Strategic Studies, 1972.
Grundy, Kenneth. *Guerrilla Struggle in Africa.* New York: Grossman Publishers, 1971.
Wilkinson, Anthony R. *Insurgency in Rhodesia, 1957-1973: An Account and Assessment.* London: International Institute for Strategic Studies, 1973.

C. EUROPE

Bell, J. Bowyer. "The Chroniclers of Violence in Northern Ireland: The First Wave Interpreted." *The Review of Politics,* Vol. 34, No. 2 (April 1972), pp. 147-157.
_____. "The Chroniclers of Violence in Northern Ireland: An Analysis of Tragedy." *The Review of Politics,* Vol. 36, No. 4 (October 1974), pp. 521-543.

————. "The Chroniclers of Violence in Northern Ireland: A Tragedy in Endless Acts." *The Review of Politics*, Vol. 38, No. 4 (October 1976), pp. 510-533.

————. *The Secret Army: The IRA, 1916-1974*. Cambridge, Massachusetts: The M.I.T. Press, 1974.

Devlin, Paddy. *The Fall of the N. I. Executive*. Belfast, Northern Ireland: Paddy Devlin, 1975.

MacStiofain, Sean. *Revolutionary in Ireland*. Edinburgh, Scotland: R & R Clark, Ltd., 1975.

O'Brien, Conor Cruise. *States of Ireland*. St. Albans, United Kingdom: Panther Books, Ltd., 1974.

Rose, Richard. *Governing Without Consensus*. Boston: Beacon Press, 1971.

————. *Northern Ireland: A Time of Choice*. New York: The Macmillan Press, Ltd., 1976.

Schmitt, David. *Violence in Northern Ireland: Ethnic Conflict and Radicalization in an International Setting*. Morristown, New Jersey: General Learning Press, 1974.

Sunday Times Insight Team. *Northern Ireland: A Report on the Conflict*. Baltimore: Penguin Books, 1972.

Tilly, Charles. "Collective Violence in European Perspective." In Hugh Davis Graham and Ted Robert Gurr (eds.), *Violence in America: Historical and Comparative Perspectives*. Washington, D.C.: National Commission on the Causes and Prevention of Violence, 1969, pp. 4-42.

Whyte, John H. "Recent Writing on Northern Ireland." *The American Political Science Review*, Vol. LXX, No. 2 (June 1976), pp. 592-596.

D. ASIA

Carnell, Francis G. "Communalism and Communism in Malaya." *Pacific Affairs*, Vol. XXVI, No. 2 (June 1953), pp. 99-117.

Fall, Bernard. *Last Reflections on a War*. New York: Doubleday and Company, Inc., 1967.

Hinton, William. *Fanshen*. New York: Monthly Review Press, 1967.

McVey, Ruth I. *The Calcutta Conference and the Southeast Asian Uprisings*. Ithaca, New York: Cornell University, Modern Indonesia Project, 1968.

O'Ballance, Edgar. *Malaya: The Communist Insurgent War, 1948-1960*. Hamden, Connecticut: Anchon Books, 1966.

Purcell, Victor. *Malaya: Communist or Free?* Stanford, California: Stanford University Press, 1954.

Pye, Lucian. *Guerrilla Communism in Malaya.* Princeton, New Jersey: The Princeton University Press, 1956.

Renick, R. Ohu. "The Emergency Regulations of Malaya: Cause and Effect." *Journal of Southeast Asian History,* Vol. VI, No. 2 (September 1965), pp. 1-39.

Thompson, Robert. *No Exit from Vietnam.* New York: David McKay Company, Inc., 1969.

Tilman, Robert. "The Non-Lessons of the Malayan Emergency," *Asian Survey,* Vol. VI, No. 8 (August 1966), pp. 407-419.

E. NORTH AMERICA

Chodos, Robert, and Nick Auf der Maur. *Quebec: A Chronicle 1968-1972.* Toronto: Canadian Journalism Foundation, 1972.

Golden, Aubrey, and Ron Haggart. *Rumours of War.* Toronto: New Press, 1971.

Hofstadter, Richard, and Michael Wallace (eds.). *American Violence.* New York: Vintage Books, 1971.

Morf, Gustave. *Terror in Quebec.* Toronto: Clark, Irwin & Company Limited, 1970.

Saywell, John. *Quebec 70.* Toronto: University of Toronto Press, 1971.

"The Weather Underground." Report of Subcommittee to Investigate the Administration of the Internal Security Act and Other Internal Security Laws of the Committee on the Judiciary, United States Senate, 94th Congress, 1st Session (1975).

F. LATIN AMERICA

Davis, Jack. *Political Violence in Latin America.* London: International Institute for Strategic Studies, 1972.

Guevara, Ernesto Ché. *The Diary of Ché Guevara.* New York: Bantam Books, 1968.

Halperin, Ernst. *Terrorism in Latin America.* Beverly Hills, California: SAGE Publications, 1976.

Jackson, Geoffrey. *Surviving the Long Night.* New York: Vanguard Press, 1974.

Johnson, Kenneth F. "On the Guatemalan Political Violence." *Politics and Society,* Vol. 4, No. 1 (Fall 1973), pp. 55-82.

Kohl, James, and John Litt. *Urban Guerrilla Warfare in Latin America.* Cambridge, Massachusetts: The M.I.T. Press, 1974.

Marighella, Carlos. "The Minimanual of the Urban Guerrilla." Appendix in Robert Moss, *Urban Guerrilla Warfare*. London: International Institute for Strategic Studies, 1971.

Porzecanski, Arturo C. *Uruguay's Tupamaros*. New York: Praeger Publishing Company, 1973.

II. International Law and Terrorism

Baumann, Carol. *The Diplomatic Kidnappings*. The Hague: Martinus Nijhoff, 1973.

Bennett, W. Tapley, Jr. "United States Initiatives in the United Nations to Combat International Terrorism." *International Lawyer*, Vol. 7, No. 4 (October 1973), pp. 752-760.

Bloomfield, Louis, and Gerald Fitzgerald. *Crimes Against International Protected Persons: Prevention and Punishment*. New York: Praeger Publishers, 1975.

Blum, Yehuda. "The Beirut Raid and the International Double Standard: A Reply to Professor Richard A. Falk." *American Journal of International Law*, Vol. LXIV, No. 1 (January 1970), pp. 73-105.

Dugard, John. "International Terrorism." *International Affairs*, Vol. 50, No. 1 (January 1974), pp. 67-81.

Falk, Richard. "The Beirut Raid and the International Law of Retaliation." *Great Issues of International Politics*, Morton Kaplan (ed.). Chicago: Aldine Publishing Company, 1970, pp. 32-61.

Golob-Nisk, Mirjana. "New Aspects of International Terrorism." *Review of International Affairs*, Vol. 26, No. 598 (1975), pp. 26-28.

Official Records of the General Assembly. 6th Committee, 27th Session, Meetings 1308-1393. New York: The United Nations, 1974.

Poulantzas, Nicholas. "Some Problems of International Law Connected with Urban Guerrilla Warfare: The Kidnapping of Members of Diplomatic Missions, Consular Offices, and Other Foreign Personnel." *Annals of International Studies*, Vol. 3 (1972), pp. 137-167.

Proceedings of the International Conference on the Repression of Terrorism. Series of League of Nations Publications, C. 94, M. 47, Legal, V.3, 1938.

Romaniecki, Leon. *The Arab Terrorists in the Middle East and the Soviet Union*. Jerusalem: The Hebrew University Soviet and East European Research Center, 1973.

Rozakis, Christos L. "Terrorism and the Internationally Protected Persons in Light of ILC's Draft Articles." *International and Comparative Law Quarterly*, Vol. 23, No. 1 (January 1974), pp. 32-72.

Sottile, Antoine. "Le Terrorisme International." *Academie de Droit Inter-national: Recueil Des Cours,* Vol. 65, 1938 (III), pp. 91-181.

Survival. "Text of the American Draft Convention on Terrorism," Vol. XV, No. 1 (January-February 1973), pp. 32-34.

III. Theoretical Literature on Political Violence

Bell, J. Bowyer. *The Myth of the Guerrilla.* New York: Alfred A. Knopf, 1971.

Black, Cyril E. and Thomas P. Thornton (eds.). *Communism and Revolu-tion: The Strategic Uses of Political Violence.* Princeton, New Jersey: Princeton University Press, 1964.

Crozier, Brian. *The Rebels: A Study of Post-War Insurrections.* London: Chatto and Windus, 1960.

Debray, Regis. *Revolution in the Revolution? Armed Struggle and Political Struggle in Latin America.* New York: Grove Press, 1967.

Eckstein, Harry (ed.). *Internal War: Problems and Approaches.* New York: The Free Press, 1966.

Evron, Yair. *The Middle East: Nations, Superpowers, and Wars.* New York: Praeger Publishers, 1973.

Fanon, Frantz. *The Wretched of the Earth.* New York: Grove Press, 1966.

Gerassi, John (ed.). *Towards Revolution,* Vols. I and II. London: Weiden-feld and Nicolson, 1971.

Guevara, Ernesto Ché. *Guerrilla Warfare.* New York: Vintage Books, 1961.

Gurr, Ted Robert. *Why Men Rebel.* Princeton, New Jersey: Princeton University Press, 1970.

Harkabi, Y. *Arab Attitudes to Israel.* New York: Hart Publishing Com-pany, Inc., 1972.

Huntington, Samuel. *Political Order in Changing Societies.* New Haven: Yale University Press, 1968.

International Institute for Strategic Studies. *Civil Violence and the Inter-national System, Part I: The Scope of Civil Violence,* and *Civil Violence and the International System, Part II: Violence and Inter-national Security.* London: International Institute for Strategic Studies, 1971.

Johnson, Chalmers. *Revolutionary Change.* Boston: Little, Brown & Company, 1966.

Laqueur, Walter. *Guerrilla.* Boston: Little, Brown & Company, 1976.

_____. *The Guerrilla Reader.* New York: Meridian Books, 1977.

_____. *The Road to Jerusalem: The Origins of the Arab-Israeli Conflict, 1967.* New York: The Macmillan Company, 1968.

Leites, Nathan, and Charles Wolf, Jr. *Rebellion and Authority: An Analytic Essay on Insurgent Conflicts*. Santa Monica, California: The RAND Corporation, 1970.

Mao Tse-tung. *On the Protracted War*. Peking: Foreign Language Press, 1954.

Moore, Barrington, Jr. *Social Origins of Dictatorship and Democracy: Lord and Peasant in the Making of the Modern World*. Boston: Beacon Press, 1966.

O'Neill, Bard. *Revolutionary Warfare in the Middle East*. Boulder, Colorado: The Paladin Press, 1974.

Paget, Julian. *Counter-Insurgency Campaigning*. London: Faber and Faber Limited, 1967.

Paret, Peter, and John W. Shy. *Guerrillas in the 1960's*. New York: Frederick A. Praeger, 1962.

Thompson, Robert. *Defeating Communist Insurgency*. New York: Frederick A. Praeger, 1966.

IV. General Literature on Terrorism

Adler, D. V., and J. H. Segre. "The Ecology of Terrorism." *Survival*, Vol. XV, No. 4 (July/August 1973), pp. 178-183.

Alexander, Yonah. *International Terrorism*. New York: AMS Press, 1976.

Bell, J. Bowyer. *Transnational Terror*. Washington, D.C.: American Enterprise Institute; Stanford, California: Hoover Institution on War, Revolution and Peace, 1975.

———. "Contemporary Revolutionary Organizations." *Transnational Relations and World Politics*. Robert O. Keohane and Joseph S. Nye, Jr. (eds.). Cambridge, Massachusetts: Harvard University Press, 1972, pp. 153-168.

Howe, Irving. "The Return of Terror." *Dissent*, Vol. 22, No. 3 (Summer 1975), pp. 227-237.

Hutchinson, Martha Crenshaw. "Transnational Terrorism and World Politics." *The Jerusalem Journal of International Relations*, Vol. 1, No. 2 (Winter 1975), pp. 109-129.

———. "Transnational Terrorism as a Policy Issue." Paper presented at the 1974 meeting of the American Political Science Association.

Jenkins, Brian. *International Terrorism: A New Mode of Conflict*. Los Angeles: Crescent Publications, 1975.

——— and Janera Johnson. *International Terrorism: A Chronology, 1968-1974*. Santa Monica, California: The RAND Corporation, R-1597-DOS/ARPA, 1975.

Laqueur, Walter. *Terrorism*. Boston: Little, Brown & Company, 1977.
_____. *The Terrorism Reader*. New York: Meridian Books, 1978.
Leurdijk, J. Henk (ed.). *International Terrorism and World Security*. New York: John Wiley & Sons, 1975.
Moss, Robert. *The War for the Cities*. New York: Coward, McCann & Geoghegan, Inc. 1972.
Pierre, Andrew J. "Coping with International Terrorism." *Survival*, Vol. XVIII, No. 2 (March/April 1976), pp. 60-67.
Possony, Stefan (ed.). *Lenin Reader*. Chicago: Henry Regnery Company, 1966.
"Terrorism." *Skeptic*. No. 11 (January/February 1976).
"Terrorism, Parts 1, 2, 3, 4." Hearings before the Committee on Internal Security, House of Representatives, 93rd Congress, 2nd Session (1974).
Trotsky, Leon. *Against Individual Terrorism*. New York: Pathfinder Press, 1974.
Walzer, Michael. "The New Terrorists." *The New Republic*, Vol. 173, No. 9 (August 30, 1975), pp. 12-14.
Wilkinson, Paul. *Political Terrorism*. New York: Halsted Press, 1975.

INDEX

ABOUT THE AUTHOR

Ernest Evans is a Research Associate at the Brookings Institution in Washington, D.C. He has contributed to *Terrorism: Interdisiplinary Perspectives* and *International Terrorism in the Contemporary World* (Greenwood Press, 1978).